A Foreigner's Guide to US Immigration

How Live, Study & Work in America

By

C. G. Jacob

Table of Contents

Chapter 1: U.S. Visa Types

The United States is seen around the world as the land of opportunity, the place to go if you want to work hard and achieve your dreams. If you are one of these people and are hoping to come to U.S. shores to study, work or eventually to become an actual U.S. citizen I am here to help you on that journey. As an immigrant myself I understand both the strong desire to live in the U.S. and also the struggle you will have to endure while working your way through the U.S. immigration process.

The truth is that the immigration process can be long and convoluted and, at times, it may seem arbitrary or cruel, but during the ups and downs of your journey keep focused on the end result: the opportunity to study, work and live in the U.S., the land where if you work hard you can do anything. There may be times during your immigration journey where you feel you will never reach your end goal, but I am here to urge you to not give up hope, to not give up on your dream. If you are a good, hardworking individual you will eventually see the fruits of your labor when you are allowed to legally work, study and live in the United States.

While on your journey I hope you can use this book as a guide to help you through at least some of the immigration maze. There is no way to document every rule and every single visa nuance in detail, but this book does hit the major visas and provides valuable information. You should still make sure to check the rules on the official United States Customs and Immigration Service (USCIS) website- http://www.uscis.gov to make sure that no regulations have changed since the production of this book.

Visa Types

Before we launch into specific visas here is a high level overview of visa types and who benefits from each visa. Let's start with the broadest way of categorizing U.S. visas. Essentially U.S. visas fall into two categories: non-immigrant or immigrant. The non-immigrant category has many different visas for many situations. The immigrant category is the same as permanent residency, known as a Green Card.

So what is a non-immigrant visa and who falls into this category? Well, a non-immigrant visa is for anyone who has to establish, while applying for their visa, that the U.S. will not be their permanent residence. They have to establish that they have a permanent residence outside of the United States and plan to return to that residence after their temporary stay in the U.S.

Here's a non-exhaustive list of non-immigrant visas so that you have an idea what is covered under this broad umbrella: H1B, E3, F1, J1, L1, TN, K1, and the B1/B2 visas. Anybody wishing to come to the U.S. on these visas will need to prove to their U.S. consular or embassy official that they have strong ties to their home country and plan to return at the end of their stay. The details of how to demonstrate "strong ties" to back home will be covered in subsequent chapters.

There is an interesting side note to this "strong ties" provision though. Both the H1B and L1 visas do allow for dual intent meaning that someone on these visas can apply for permanent residency status via their employer while they are in the U.S. working under these visas. Also, the E3 does seem to allow applications for permanent residency as well even though this rule is never explicitly stated in the regulations.

The immigrant visa category is much simpler. It is essentially permanent residency and these visas fall under three categories.

- Family Sponsored (direct relatives only)
- Employer Sponsored
- Special Categories

The people applying for these visas are applying for Green Cards and do not need to prove any ties to home since their intention is to reside in the U.S. permanently. The details of these visas will be covered in Chapter 7 on Green Cards (inc. EB or Employment Based visas).

Before we launch into more detail on different visa types I should call out that the fiscal year for all visas starts on October 1 and ends on September 30 of the following year. This fact is essential to understand, especially for H1B visa and Green Card applicants.

Non-immigrant Visas

This section is going to list and very briefly describe many of the non-immigrant visas. The most popular visas will be covered in subsequent chapters in more detail. If you need more information about some of the more obscure visas please visit http://www.usicis.gov.

The H Visa Temporary Worker

There are several H visa categories for temporary workers.

- H1B- for professionals coming to work in specialty occupations
- H1C- for professional nurses
- H2A- for agricultural workers
- H2B- for non-agricultural workers (unskilled foreign workers)
- H3- for trainees

The E Visa

E visas are for nationals of certain countries where there is a trade treaty between the U.S. and the other country.

- E1- for an individual who is doing substantial trade with the U.S.
- E2- for investors who are directing an investment
- E3- for Australian citizens only (a working visa similar to H1B)

The L Visa Temporary Worker

The L visa is for a foreign national generally at the managerial level to transfer internally in a subsidiary of a multi-national company.

- L1A- for a manager or executive
- L1B- for someone with specialized knowledge

Student & Training Visas

- F1- for students to study full time at an academic institution such as a university or language school
- J1- for people coming to the U.S. to work or train with an organization that has been approved for an exchange program under the J1 regulations (also is used for High School exchange programs)
- M- for individuals looking to attend an approved course of study leading to a specific vocational or educational objective

Temporary Visas for Specific Occupations

- O1- for foreign nationals who have demonstrated an extraordinary or high achievement in the sciences, arts, education, business or athletics whose achievements have been recognized in their field
- O2- for support staff of the foreign national receiving an O1 visa

P Visa for Athletes and Artists

- P1- for an athlete and/or athletic teams and entertainment groups
- P2- for artists and entertainer reciprocal exchange
- P3- for artists and entertainers integral to a specific performance

Other Non-immigrant Visas

- TN Visa- for certain qualifying Canadian and Mexican citizens to work temporarily in the U.S. under NAFTA (North American Free Trade Agreement) rules
- Q1 Visa- for a foreign national to obtain practical training or employment and for the sharing of the history and culture of a his home country
- R1 Visa- for a foreign national with a religious profession to work in the U.S. on a temporary basis
- B1- for business professionals to travel to the U.S. for short term business purposes such as conferences
- B2- for tourists to travel to and enjoy the U.S. before returning home.

Immigrant Visas

Immigrant visas are generally referred to as Permanent Residency Status or Green Cards. These visas are for people that plan to remain in the U.S. permanently. The Employment Based (EB) visas, as they are also called, are for lawful permanent residents who fall under five preference categories.

- EB1- Priority Workers (people with extraordinary ability, outstanding professors or researchers, and intra-company transfers of executives)
- EB2- Professionals holding advanced degrees or persons of exceptional ability
- EB3- Skilled workers, professionals and other workers
- EB4- Special immigrants, including religious workers and ministers
- EB5- Investors with the potential to hire 10 U.S. workers

Partner Visas

Partner visas are companion visas that are meant to bring spouses or dependents of primary visa holders to the U.S. as well. Most of the visas mentioned above do have a partner visa. Some will allow the spouse or dependent to work and/or study in the U.S., but some will not. The exact regulations surrounding each partner visa do differ so you should research the specific rules for whichever visa your dependents will be on.

Some of the visas above that have accompanying partner visas are: H1B (H4), F1 (F2), J1 (J2) (in some circumstances), E3 (E3D), L1 (L2), and the EB category.

So in closing, as you can see there are many U.S. visas. There are also many regulations surrounding each one of these visas and it will behoove you to learn about the specific one you may qualify for before you even begin the application process.

The remainder of this book covers several of the more popular visas in much more detail. Hopefully the information will help make the entire process much easier to understand. If you still have some questions after reading everything I suggest two ways to find more information. First, consult the U.S. immigration website as mentioned earlier- http://www.uscis.gov and second, if necessary, consult an immigration lawyer who specializes in your immigration situation.

Good luck with your immigration journey and I hope this book can help you on your way!

Chapter 2: F1 Visa

The F1 visa is one of the most popular non-immigrant visas. It is the standard visa for all students who wish to study at a U.S. college or university at any level. It is so popular for two basic reasons. First, the post-secondary education in the U.S. is one of he best in the world. There are truly top tier universities like Harvard or Yale, but there are also many more excellent universities in the tiers under these elite schools. There are so many colleges and universities that truly give students a top notch education.

The second reason this visa is so popular is that F1 students can leverage some short term work programs to help them obtain an H1B visa through their employer. In other words, the F1 visa is one of the best ways to come to the U.S. to study and then stay permanently by transferring to an H1B, E3 or other work related visa. Many students still see the U.S. as the land of opportunity and hope by working hard they will be able to succeed on a grand scale.

So now that we've covered what the F1 is for and why it is so popular let's delve into the requirements you need to fulfill in order to get this visa.

F1 Visa Requirements

The requirements for the F1 visa are very straightforward and, unlike some other visas, easy to follow.

1. You must be fully proficient in English. Like I said, very straightforward. There are a few exceptions to this rule such as if you are attending an English language school for the express purpose to learn and become fluent in English this pre-requisite does not hold. Also, some universities may make an exception and allow you to take a few extra English classes, but this is rare so don't bet on it. You will need to prove you're proficient so you will probably be required to

take an entrance exam or submit ample documentation to prove your English ability. Basically if you speak and write English well this requirement will not be an issue.

2. You have to prove you have sufficient funds to both pay for the education and your living expenses. You will need to prove that these funds exist before receiving final USCIS (United States Customs and Immigration Service) approval and before starting your course of study at a college. Obviously the exact amount of money you will need depends on the college you choose and where it is located. Living expenses in New York City are much higher than a town in the middle of Ohio. Plus private universities are more expensive than public state universities. Unless you receive a scholarship you will generally have to pay large tuition fees up front for an undergraduate degree so be prepared.

3. The institution has to be approved by the USCIS. Most U.S. colleges and universities were approved a long time ago so it will generally be easy to meet this requirement. Sometimes some new, obscure, schools have not been approved yet, but those are a very small minority of cases.

4. The institution that will be sponsoring you must issue you an I-120A-B form which is essentially their stated satisfaction that you meet all the requirements such as funding, English competency and all academic pre-requisites.

So that's it. The F1 visa process is easy. The hardest part is getting admitted to a university and making sure you have the funds. Universities in the U.S. are much more expensive than in other parts of the world so be prepared for a shock when you see the price. This fact is especially true for undergraduate programs as there are fewer scholarships or government based grants available for bachelor's degrees. For master's degrees though, especially in areas like engineering, computer science, math, and other hard sciences there are many programs that will cover the cost of tuition plus provide a small stipend for living expenses. If you are able to get into a university program that will pay your education expenses, you will not be wealthy, but it will help immensely.

At the PhD level you generally have to be invited by the university to continue your education so the tuition and most fees are usually covered. You will also typically be given a small stipend for living expenses just like with a master's degree. Be aware that this stipend will probably not cover all your living expenses though.

Although the F1 visa is a very popular route to getting to and working in the U.S., it is not an inexpensive route by any means. You will need to either earn a scholarship or have a rather large budget to afford to study on an F1 visa in the U.S.

U.S. Student Life

Once you're made it to the U.S. on an F1 visa you will get to experience life as a U.S. student. Life for the student in the U.S. to a large extent is whatever you want it to be. There are so many colleges and universities and in every location imaginable that you can really find a way to study and explore your interests no matter what subjects are your passion. Most schools will have many sports teams, both for the expert athlete and the novice. There are theater and arts extracurricular programs as well and political and religious groups. Many of the larger universities will also have ethnic groups that cater to immigrants of all countries. There are of course frequent parties on many campuses and these are not hard to find. That being said, student life is not all about partying or goofing around. Most of the institutions are quite good and you will have to study hard in order to maintain good grades and stay in school. Do not make the mistake of thinking that getting in is the hardest part. You will have to find a way to balance the hard work with the fun if you want to maintain your visa and ultimately receive your degree.

Working while on an F1 Visa

One great advantage of the F1 visa is that the visa holder is allowed to work legally through several avenues. The student may work on campus part-time, usually through a university work program. This type of a job does not count towards any of their allotted time to work in the U.S. that some of the other F1 work programs have as restrictions.

The second avenue that students can use is called the Curricular Practical Training (CPT). As mentioned briefly in chapter 6 about E3 visas, this program is designed to help the foreign student obtain work experience by working in a job off campus that is in their field of study. You may use your job under the CPT program as a way to earn credits while also earning a salary. Be aware though that if you work more than 12 months under the CPT program you will be ineligible for the Occupational Practical Training (OPT) following graduation. Permission to work in the CPT program is granted via the International Students Office or similar body at your institution.

Now onto the Occupational Practical Training Program (OPT). In my opinion the OPT program is one of the biggest advantages of the F1 visa. OPT allows undergraduates, post graduation, to work up to one year for a U.S. company and students with advanced degrees to work up to two years, thereby giving these students the ability to find an employer, prove their value, and also check out the U.S. work environment while hopefully convincing their employer to sponsor them for an H1B visa. What a great deal!

Let's walk through the process and filing costs for OPT. This process is also amazingly straightforward and easy to follow, but there are some fees attached. I have to say though that considering the process and costs for the H1B visa, the F1 OPT is easy and cheap!

Here are the 5 simple steps.

1. Request the Designated School Official (DSO) at your university to approve your request for an OPT position. The DSO can deny this request, but will rarely do so if the student has a legitimate offer and it is in the student's field of study.
2. The DSO will note the OPT position on the student's I-20 form and update the SEVIS (Student and Exchange Visitor Information System) records.

3. The foreign student then files form I-765 with the USCIS which costs $340 and is paid by the student.
4. The I-765 (Application for an Employment Authorization Document (EAD)) and is issued if the USCIS approves the work position. It is rare that a position that is in your field of study is denied so don't be worried about that.

One key thing to note about the CPT in conjunction with the OPT is that however long you worked on the CPT program will be deducted from the amount of time you have for OPT. Make sure you have a plan for after graduation if you ultimately want to stay in the U.S.

The OPT STEM Extension

On April 8, 2008, an interim order came from the Department of Homeland Security allowing certain students to apply for up to a 17 month extension of their OPT work giving them up to a maximum of 29 months of being able to work under this status. This temporary, interim ruling was designed to provide a solution to what is known as the H1B visa "cap-gap". This "cap-gap" is when a student's F1 visa status and EAD period has expired during a U.S. immigration fiscal year (Oct. 1 – Sept. 30), but prior to their being eligible to work under an approved H1B visa, starting on Oct. 1st.

An example of this gap is if a student is approved for an H1B visa on May 15th, but their OPT time runs out on August 1st. Under the H1B visa they are not allowed to start work for their employer until Oct. 1st, but they also can no longer work under their OPT status. The foreign student would have to leave the country and return to start work for Oct. 1st. This situation hurts both the employer and the student. (More details on the H1B visa are given in chapter 5.)

So why is this interim order called the STEM extension? Well, this extension is intended for foreign students that have graduated in areas designated as important to the U.S. economy with many open positions, but a constant shortage of U.S. citizen graduates. These designated areas are: Science, Technology, Engineering, and Mathematics (STEM). Under STEM the eligible degree fields are:

- Computer Science Applications

- Biological and Biomedical Sciences

- Actuarial Science

- Mathematics and Statistics

- Engineering

- Military Technologies

- Engineering Technologies

- Physical Sciences

- Science Technologies

- Medical Scientist

Please note that your extension approval will be based on these types of degrees. If you have an undergraduate degree in engineering, but a graduate degree in history and your OPT is based on your graduate degree then you are not eligible for a STEM extension. Conversely, if your undergraduate degree is in history, but your graduate degree is in engineering and your OPT is based on that engineering degree you are eligible.

You should also be aware that it is mandatory for your employer to be enrolled in the free U.S. government E-verify program and that you apply for your STEM extension prior to the expiration of your current OPT period. If these two criteria are not met you will not be eligible for the extension.

STEM Extension Process and Costs

As with almost everything involving the U.S. immigration system there is a process and a cost to the STEM extension. Luckily the process for the STEM 17 month extension is pretty painless. The cost, although not huge, is not painless in my opinion.

Here is the process:

- The foreign student must file Form I-765 with the USCIS which again costs $340 U.S.D. You must also include with your filing your I-20 endorsed by the DSO at your institution and then a copy of your degree in one of the designated STEM fields of study. You are effectively amending your original I-765 as well as including this information in your employer's E-verify information.

- If there is a delay in granting your 17 month extension and you filed the STEM extension ahead of time, you can obtain an employment authorization extension for up to 180 days so that you will not be out of status.

Once you obtain your STEM extension you will be required to report every 6 months to your DSO information regarding your employer and your status in terms of address, contacts, and names. Also, if any of this information ever changes you need to report these changes within 10 days.

One more, great thing about the STEM extension is if the extension expires before Oct. 1st and you have an approved H1B visa petition then you are automatically granted a work authorization extension up to Oct. 1st for when your H1B status takes effect. If this is your situation make sure to continue to file with your DSO every 6 months though.

OPT Program Authorized Work Categories

Now that the process and costs surrounding the OPT program and STEM extension have been covered let's talk about the categories of work that you are allowed to engage in while in the OPT program. This section is not about a particular type of job, but rather the work parameters around that job. (Please note that you may not be able to apply for a STEM extension for some of these categories.)

- Paid employment – Students may work part time (at least 20 hours per week) or full time.

- Multiple employers – Students may work for more than one employer, but all their positions must be related to their degree and for CPT cannot exceed the cumulative hours allowed per week.

- Short term multiple employers (performing artists) – Students, such as musicians or performing artists, may work for multiple short term employers (gigs). The student must maintain a list of all engagements, dates and duration. They must be prepared to show a list of all engagements if requested by DHS.

- Work for hire: This category is often referred to as 1099 employment where an individual performs a service based on a contractual relationship. The student is not technically "employed" by the employer as far as the IRS is concerned. If requested by DHS a full list and evidence of this work must be provided. There may be additional tax implications under this arrangement so make sure to review the IRS's regulations.

- Self-employed business owner – Students on OPT are actually allowed to start their own business and be self-employed. In this situation the student must work full time and must be able to prove that he or she has the proper business licenses and is actively engaged in a business related to the student's degree program.

- Employment through an agency – Students on post graduation OPT can work through an agency, but must be able to show evidence that they worked an average of at least 20 hours per week while employed by the agency.

- Unpaid employment – Students may work as volunteers or unpaid interns, as long as no labor laws are violated. They must work at least 20 hours per week if they are on post graduation OPT. These students must also be able to provide evidence from their employer if required by DHS.

As a quick last note on the F1 visa, there is currently pending legislation to give foreign students with U.S. graduate degrees or higher, particularly for those in the STEM disciplines, an automatic and quicker route to a Green Card. Also, as you finish your degree be aware that there is also pending legislation to provide an easier route to permanent residency for entrepreneurs. In brief, if you can get venture capitalist or angel investor backing and you are able to hire 5 U.S. based employees after 2 years of being in business you may be eligible for a very quick path to permanent residency.

F2 Partner Visa

As with many visa categories, the F1 visa has a partner visa – the F2. The F2 visa is for spouses and dependents. The basics of the F2 visa is that spouses cannot work or study on the F2 visa. School age children may attend school, but it must be elementary or secondary school (Kindergarten through 12th grade). For a dependent to enroll in and attend a college or university they must have their own F1visa.

As with many partner visas, the F2 visa holder's status is dependent on the principal F1 holder's status. If the F1 holder becomes out of status, then his or her dependents on the F2 visa are out of status as well.

Pros and Cons of the F1 Visa

As stated earlier in this chapter, the F1 visa is very popular as it is a great way to come to the U.S. to study and get a foothold in the country while you look for employment and eventually long term permanent resident status. This section is meant to give a quick view of the Pros and Cons of the F1 visa so that you can see the good and the bad associated with this status.

Pros

- You earn a U.S. degree or certificate which is well respected around the world.

- You participate in campus life which opens up tons of networking opportunities

- You can transfer from one school to another merely by filing the change with the USCIS.

- You can work part time on campus and have access to the CPT and OPT programs.

- You can travel freely in and out of the U.S. as long as your visa is valid and your I-20 form is signed by the institution.

- You can bring your dependents on the F2 visa.

- You can generally stay as long as it takes to complete your studies and can extend your F1 status relatively easily.

- It is fairly easy to transfer to an H1B or E3 visa as long as you find an employer willing to sponsor you.

- The U.S. is the largest economy in the world and being in the U.S. to search for a job is a big leg up in the job search game.

Cons

- You cannot work legally off campus while still a student unless the institution approves. It can be hard to get approval as you often need to prove economic hardship.

- If you do work off campus, as many people do, it may be more difficult to obtain a Green Card later in life.

- Your dependents cannot work on the F2 visa and your spouse cannot attend school. Dependent children, under age 21, may attend school, but only on the elementary or secondary levels. They must obtain their own F1 visa to attend university.

- You cannot apply for a Green Card directly from an F1 visa.

- The cost of U.S. education is very high and unless you are granted a scholarship you will have to pay each year's tuition upfront.

F1 Visa vs. the M1 Visa

Before ending this chapter on the F1 visa let's quickly discuss the M1 visa and how it differs from the F1 visa. Just like the F1 visa the M1 is intended for students. The big difference is that the M1 is intended for non-academic or vocational courses. Essentially the M1 visa is meant for candidates who wish to study in the U.S. in order to increase their vocational skills. The only other real difference between these visas is the I-20 form that must be filed. For the F1 the candidate must file Form I-10 A-B while the M1 candidate must file Form I-20M-N. Besides that the two visas are quite similar.

The M1 visa candidate must provide a valid passport, any necessary transcripts or diplomas, and of course, proof that they can pay for their studies and also their living expenses while in the country. Essentially they need to prove that they will not be a financial burden to the U.S., not surprising given U.S. immigration policies.

The M1 visa also has a partner visa, the M2, that works just like the F2. On the M2, spouses may not work or attend school, but school age children may attend elementary or secondary school.

So that's pretty much it. The two visas are very similar and really only differ on the type of course work the applicant is planning to study.

That's the end of the F1 chapter. I hope it was helpful. In the next chapters we will begin the discussion about how to find a job in the U.S. and how to apply for and receive an employment based visa.

Chapter 3: How to Find a Job in U.S.

If you've decided that you want to find a job in the U.S., how do you start? Well, the first thing to consider is moving to the U.S. Yes, it is an expense and can be risky, but most employers are reluctant to hire someone sight unseen. They are also unlikely to even grant a phone interview if your phone number has a country code outside the U.S. It is possible to set up a U.S. phone number via Skype or Google Voice, but then you must be prepared to answer the phone during normal American business hours which, given time zone differences, can be in the middle of the night.

Even if you manage to have a great phone interview while you are outside the U.S., the employer will usually expect to hold a follow up face to face interview within a few days. If you are not able to physically get to the location of your interview within a few days, the employer may not be willing to wait.

Although there is an expense and some risk involved in coming to the U.S. before you have a job, it is often the far better way to approach your job search. You do need to do some planning though.

Lodging

First, focus on lodging. Do you have a friend or relative that you can live with while you look for a job? If not, research the area you plan to live in while you look for work and budget how much a hotel or hostel would cost. You may be able to find an apartment to rent, but that will depend on the landlord. Most landlords will want to run a background and credit check on their tenants and to do that in the U.S. a social security number is needed. Being a foreigner you will not be able to apply for a social security number until you have accepted a job offer. There are some landlords that will not do the usual background checks, but the apartments these landlords are renting may not be in locations you'd chose for your worst enemies.

There are a couple of good options that circumvent the usual background check process though so don't despair that your lodging will have to be in a hotel or hostel if you do not know anyone in the United States. You can look to sublet a place. The best way to find sublets in the U.S. is by using Craigslist (www.craigslist.org). Once on Craigslist pull up the city you are looking to move to and search under the sublets/temporary or rooms/shared sections. Of course before you officially decide on a sublet make sure to meet the person you will be subletting from.

Another good resource for finding lodging is Airbnb (www.airbnb.com). This website provides a great service where you can search for housing or an extra room anywhere in the world, negotiate the price and usually find a place to stay without going through a full blown background check. It is truly a wonderful resource that can help out so many people.

Transportation

Public transportation in big cities is generally good, but outside of the big cities most Americans travel by car. That being said please note that by big cities I mean places like New York City, San Francisco, Washington D.C. and Chicago. If you are looking to move to smaller cities like Boston or Philadelphia there is still decent public transportation, but it will not get you everywhere at all times. Also, amazingly enough, Los Angeles has a pretty poor public transportation system. Wherever you are thinking of settling make sure to check out public transportation via the Internet if you do not want to buy or lease a car. All the major cities will have online maps and schedules to help you understand the train, subway and bus systems.

Food and Other Budget Items

Also consider your budget for food, any additional clothes you may need for the interviewing process and of course any other basic living items you will need. Food in the U.S. is overall inexpensive compared to most other countries so that expense shouldn't surprise you. Clothes are also less expensive in the U.S. than in other parts of the world. Of course the cost for all of the basic necessities of life will change based on where you will be living. Everything is more expensive in places like New York or Washington, D.C. than in the middle of Oklahoma.

Healthcare

Be aware that healthcare costs are high and without U.S. based health insurance you will have to pay the full cost of any medical needs you have. Once you get a job, you may be able to get health insurance through your employer, which although not inexpensive, will help. I'll discuss more about the topic of health insurance and healthcare later.

U.S. Resume

Once you've decided to move to the U.S. (or not), it's time to work on your U.S. style resume. There are plenty of websites that will charge you to help you Americanize your resume, but for the most part those services aren't needed. In this highly global world, where labor constantly travels from country to country, the differences among resumes (language aside) truly aren't that vast. Resumes are becoming more homogenized across the international labor market every day.

Even though there is more to landing a job than your resume it is still a very important first step and is often the first impression that any potential employer has of you so here are the major points of a U.S. style resume. Depending on the industry these factors may vary, but these points are the standard to cover for most professions.

General Points to Consider
- It is best to keep it to a single page. If you have additional portfolio or other items of interest send those examples as additions.
- Put it in reverse chronological order, i.e. list your most recent experience first then your education and then any extra information.

- Put all of your contact details in the header so as not to waste space.
- Consider adding a one to two sentence summary of your key abilities and strengths just prior to your work experience. Tailor your summary to the position to which you are applying.
- In work experience, list your most recent experience first. List the company name and location, job title, and dates of service for each position you have held. Under each position use a bulleted list of your key responsibilities. Keep these bullets short and straight to the point such as "managed $10 million marketing budget for clients across all channels".
- Under your education state the institution, all relevant qualifications achieved and your year of graduation. If an explanation of any of your qualifications or awards is needed then add that here as well. You may consider listing the website for the institution in case your interviewer wishes to learn more.
- After education you can list any additional skills, achievements or awards and personal interests you think are relevant; however, this is not the focus of the resume so keep it brief.
- Next you may list some reference check names and contact details. Some U.S. companies will check your references, some will not. Most companies will also have a section on their job application for this information so if your resume is running long you may wish to omit this section.
- The last section of your resume should pertain to your Visa status. I recommend that you be upfront with potential employers and let them know you need their sponsorship. Here are some examples of verbiage you may consider using:
  - *I am eligible to work under the H1B visa which runs for 3 years and is renewable and transferrable.*

- *I am eligible to work under the J1 visa which is designed for internships for foreign workers.*
- *As an Australian I am eligible for the E3 visa which is specifically for Australian professionals working for U.S. employers. (This visa works similarly to the Canadian TN Visa and requires 1 form, the Labor Condition Application (LCA- U.S. State Dept., Info) be completed.)*

If you have a mentor or friend who is used to the U.S. job market consider having him or her review your resume to ensure it follows the standards of the U.S. resume. It is important that your resume be in the expected format so that you are measured on your qualifications, not on your resume writing skills.

The truth is that even when you have a killer resume you will probably have to go beyond your resume to obtain a job offer and eventually obtain your E3 or H1B work visa. Basically it will be the whole package, your presentation, extra efforts and interview performance that will ultimately get you a job offer.

The Job Search

Once your resume is completed your official job search can begin. The first thing to note is that a job search in the U.S. is very much like a job search in your home country. You will use many of the same methods so the process will not be intimidating. The hardest part of landing that job is that you have to convince a company twice, once to hire you and then again to sponsor you. Often the most difficult part is convincing a company to sponsor you. Many will reject you from the outset based on the fact that you are not a U.S. citizen or resident able to work without sponsorship. In my opinion, the best way to approach this problem is to be honest about your visa status from the beginning. It will do you no good to hide the fact that you need sponsorship until far down the interview path as let's face it, an employer that is not open to sponsorship will not become more open to the idea later down the road and may even resent being kept in the dark. Even though some companies will not be willing to sponsor you there are many that will.

To be fair, there is another school of thought though that believes the best approach is to convince a prospective employer that you are an outstanding candidate and then later in the process divulge that sponsorship is required. There is no guaranteed right approach. The first approach of being upfront about your status will avoid heartache in the cases where you get a job offer only to uncover that the employer will not sponsor you. The second approach avoids your being rejected solely based on your immigration status. Some people believe that if you are a good candidate then the employer will change their mind after they meet and interview you. I again believe that the first approach is preferable, but how you handle the situation is completely at your discretion.

The easiest and most likely way to find a job and sponsorship in the U.S. is via an internal transfer within your current company or through word of mouth. The people in charge of the hiring decision will already be aware of your visa status, plus as with applying at home, you are already a known quantity. Hopefully you are highly recommended which will make you a less risky commodity and an employer will be much more willing to take the risk and sponsor your visa so keep your eyes and ears open.

If your current employer or the stakeholder companies you deal with have a U.S. office talk to people in management, HR and your everyday colleagues. Try to feel out if there are any opportunities to transfer.

At the same time join some networking and business groups that attract Americans in your area. Rotary and local Chamber of Commerce groups usually attract expat Americans as do many religious and cultural organizations. Get to know the people in these groups and see if they know of any opportunities. Similarly let every relative and friend with any possible connection to the U.S. know of your interest in finding a job over here. Online groups like Meetup.com and LinkedIn can also help, but they are best used in conjunction with the other suggestions above.

While you are networking with people, also begin looking at online jobs sites. Although there are many good jobs sites catering to all fields the four best sites, in my opinion, are:

1. Monster.com
2. LinkedIn.com
3. Craigslist.org
4. ZipRecruiter.com

These sites are easy to use and apply through, send the least email SPAM and have a steady stream of good positions every day. Other sites like CareerBuilder.com send too much email SPAM and are not nearly as easy to use. Hot Jobs and Google Jobs just don't have the volume of jobs to make them worthwhile.

Another site called TheLadders.com has positions with salaries above $100K U.S.D only, but you have to pay to see their listings. If you are in this salary range then I recommend you check it out.

Recruiters are another good avenue for finding a U.S. based job. They are a large part of the U.S. job search in all industries and for almost all levels of job positions. If you are at a high ability in your field, recruiters may reach out and contact you directly. If so, definitely work with them. They can be one of the best ways into a company without a referral.

If you are not contacted directly by recruiters, don't be afraid to contact them directly. If you have applied to positions via the online job sites you may also get call backs from recruiters. Many of the postings online are from recruiters looking to fill a position. LinkedIn is also a great way to contact recruiters online and then set up a time to talk to them about your qualifications.

How ever you contact a recruiter be prepared to describe your expertise and your unique selling points. Remember that in the U.S. you should always Sell Sell Sell Yourself! If the recruiter does not understand the value you add they will not be willing to present your resume to perspective employers. You must convince the recruiter that you have the skills and the ability that employers are seeking.

All of the above mainstream methods for your job search are excellent and should be explored. At the same time don't discount the less obvious avenues for seeking employment. Look in smaller, local newspapers, trade magazines, on church bulletin boards and even on public bulletin boards in grocery stores. These places may not have the volume of jobs listed as online resources and recruiters do, but there will also be much fewer people applying for these positions.

Another piece of advice while applying for jobs is to stay focused on a niche industry and apply to all the jobs you can find in that industry either through online jobs sites, recruiters or word of mouth. By focusing on an industry you will quickly learn everything there is to know about it and every position that may be open. You will also learn all the companies in your niche giving you a huge advantage during interviews. If you spread yourself across many industry segments you run the risk of getting lost and not being able to communicate effectively why you are the right fit for a position.

To add to this last tip try to focus your job search in a growing sector for the U.S. economy. Five key sectors that appear to be growing even in today's climate are: IT, Health, Education, Online and New Energy. Each of these sectors has a lot of money flowing into it, is growing rapidly and requires a wide range of skills from marketing to engineering to medical.

Let's delve into each of these sectors in a little more detail. The IT industry has been booming for over a decade now and there is no reason to think it won't continue growing in the foreseeable future. Why? Well, technology is the fabric of life to companies now. Every single company out there has to have a technology footprint even if they are too small to have an internal IT department. Without computers and other technologies companies just don't run anymore. Obviously the best way into the IT sector is by having a degree (or equivalent experience) in some form of computer science or information technology. If you don't have a degree in these fields you can still get your foot in the door by taking some basic computer programming or related classes. If you can prove to a company that you have some basic technology skills and the aptitude you can often find a job as there are not enough qualified Americans to fill the positions.

The Health sector of the American economy is also still growing mostly due to the fact that the U.S. population is growing older, meaning that a larger proportion of Americans are now becoming senior citizens. Health care is also becoming more technology based and more sophisticated which adds more jobs as well. If you are looking to enter the Health sector as a caregiver you will need a degree or some sort of certification. If you are, however, interested in working in the sector in a more supporting role such as marketing or accounting, believe me those jobs are plentiful and are in need of intelligent workers.

Education is an interesting sector as it is growing, largely due to some federal laws that mandate certain levels of student aptitude, but it is at the same time being squeezed by the economic slowdown and loss in tax revenues. That being said, Americans see themselves as very pro education and for that reason alone this sector has continued to grow. If you do not have teacher certification for the state you are planning to work in then consider becoming certified as a teacher's assistant, applying for teaching positions at smaller or community colleges, or looking for a position as an education administrator at a school, college or university. Again, this is an industry that is always in need of qualified applicants.

One of the hottest sectors in the U.S. is anything having to do with the Internet. Everything is now online and if you have a business, but no website, you probably aren't doing all that much business. Yes, a lot of the jobs associated with the Internet are technology based, but companies also need website designers, artists, editors, copywriters and even marketers to help them develop a strong and beneficial online presence. To get into the online world you will just need to prove that you can add value to the company's online portfolio or strategy. Remember that people to help coordinate and manage all of the moving parts are also in great demand so don't sell yourself short even if you aren't a techie or an artist.

The last hot sector that we'll discuss is New Energy, or what many in the U.S. call Green Energy. This sector is one of the hottest industries as the U.S. government is constantly pouring money into it looking for new and novel ways to reduce American dependence on foreign energy, namely oil. Even with the global recession there is not much evidence that this trend will end anytime soon. A great thing about this sector is that it needs people to handle every aspect of business from accounting to marketing to public relations. Whatever your degree or work experience it is highly likely that you can use it to qualify for a job in the New Energy industry.

So what if you don't want to work in these sectors or for some reason really feel that you're not qualified? Don't worry you can work in any sector in the U.S. These sectors are just some of the hottest and fastest growing right now so opportunities are more abundant in these. If you want to work in a different industry though, then go find that perfect job for you. And don't be worried that your degree won't fill the requirements for your visa. For the most part the American undergraduate system is much more general than the rest of the world and it is not uncommon for someone with a degree in Political Science to go to work for a big bank doing some finance function. You will just have to explain your choices and how they relate to your job opportunity at your consulate interview. Keep your explanation high level and explain that you have a passion or talent for the position and that your education lays a foundation for the role you will be filling.

One last thing to keep in mind when looking for a U.S. based job is that many people focus on the big areas such as New York, Chicago and California as they see these as the most desirable places to live. They can be nice locations, but remember that they also have some of the highest taxes and costs of living. Other parts of the country are desperate for workers and may allow your take home salary to be higher in the end. Plus it may be easier to get a green card from a "less desirable" location.

The U.S. Interview

Once you've applied for a position and the potential employer is highly impressed by your new U.S. style resume, the next stage is often a phone interview. The phone interview may be impromptu, but is often set for a particular date and time. It is typically briefer than an in person interview and will cover the more general things about your background and resume. The interviewer will often share information pertaining to the company and the position itself. Although most phone interviews are fairly basic, be prepared to talk about anything in your education or work history and to discuss why you are a good fit for the position.

One thing that is different in U.S. interviews from interviews in many other countries is that questions relating to compensation tend to come up early. Be prepared to discuss what you want to be paid even if you are not used to this in interviews back home. It may even come up during the phone interview.

Some good advice is to research average salaries for your position and geographical location online so that you know the going rates. Decide on the amount you wish to seek and then add $10K as it is always better to aim high. Remember, you will not get more than you originally state. You can always allow yourself to be negotiated down a little. Be American and demand more for yourself.

Assuming you pass the phone interview expect to be invited in for a face to face interview. This interview will generally be within a few days of the phone interview so you can see that it is important to already be in the U.S. Most in person interviews will be with multiple people, either separately or in a group setting. They are most often conducted in a series of one on one interviews, but be prepared for a group interview as well. You may not know exactly how the interview process will work within individual companies until you are onsite at the company.

During the face to face interviews each interviewer will ask more detailed questions about your skills, job experience and education. They will be trying to gauge how well you can handle the work, but will also be assessing how well your personality will mess with the overall team. It is important to U.S. companies that you are able to fit in and work well with a team. If they feel you will be difficult to get along with they will not hire you.

Be aware that in some industries, especially high tech industries, your interviewers may be dressed in regular street clothes like jeans and a t-shirt. Even though they may be dressed in casual clothes you should always dress the part. It never hurts to overdress, but being underdressed can come across as if you are too casual or don't take the interview seriously.

If you feel you are getting to the final stages of the interview process or are applying for a senior position do not be afraid to ask to be reimbursed for your travel expenses. It is almost expected at certain levels that you will be compensated for your expenses. Of course, in most cases, you are not going to be reimbursed for plane tickets from your home country to the U.S., but travel within the U.S. is often compensated. It never hurts to ask for the compensation and if you do not get the job it is at least some consolation that your expenses were covered by the company.

When the interviews are complete always leave on a good note. If you are not their first choice candidate, but are second or third in line it is still possible that the person offered the job will decline. If that happens they will often offer the position to the next person in line and if you left on a bad note that will not be you.

Always be prepared to discuss the details of your contract so that when that job offer comes you will be able to handle any details. Most contracts will have a probationary period, often for 90 days. During your probationary period essentially the company can fire you with no compensation other than what you have worked thus far and they don't have to give you a reason.

After this initial probationary period, you will be an "at will" employee meaning that you can still be fired on the spot with no notice, but you will probably get a payout for unused leave and possibly other termination compensation depending on the circumstances.

The U.S. system of termination is brutal so don't expect two weeks notice or even cordiality if it happens. From the moment you are fired you are considered a security risk and they won't be able to get you out of the building fast enough. Although it is not personal, it can be very difficult to experience or even watch.

Most companies will include medical/dental/vision insurance, life insurance and retirement as part of the employment package. Make sure you know what benefits are included. Since medical insurance is super expensive and annoying to deal with you especially want to make sure that is included. It will still be a hassle, but at least most of the expense will be covered.

You've Got the Job! Now What?

Once you've received a job offer and accepted it then celebrate! Give yourself a pat on the back. Then focus on getting your visa process underway. Here are the six steps to follow to go from the job offer to officially starting work at your new position.

1. Have the employer fill out the sponsorship document(s) and pay the relevant filing fees - The first step is to have your employer fill out the sponsorship document and pay the relevant filing fees. The fees will depend on the type of visa you need. You can also fill out the forms, pay for the visa and have your employer submit everything, but if your sponsor is a reputable company they will usually handle all of it through their attorney. The details for filing for an H1B or E3 visa will be discussed in subsequent chapters.

2. Understand your dates - Next you have to understand your dates for filing your visa paperwork. This process is very straightforward for an E3 visa, but more complicated for an H1B visa. With an H1B visa there is an annual filing date of April 1 and a hard quota as well. Even if your H1B visa is approved you cannot start employment until October 1st of that year.

3. Schedule your interview – Once you have or anticipate having your visa documents from your employer, have completed the forms you need to fill out and have all the fees, photos and other proof documents you will need to schedule your interview with the U.S. Consulate. Make sure that the consulate you contact can process your visa type. Each country and sometimes city has different wait times and processes so be prepared and learn about the consulate you will work with.
4. Book your ticket – Schedule your flight back to the U.S. and be prepared to answer potential questions at your port of entry into the U.S. If you have all your papers in order you will be fine although it can seem intense depending on the official with whom you are dealing.
5. Get a Social Security Number (SSN) – A social security number is essential for living in the United States. It is used for everything from opening a bank account, getting a credit card, signing a lease and getting paid. You can only get a SSN from within the country and it can take up to eight weeks for the government to process and send you a card.
6. Start Work! – That's it. Congratulations! You are now ready to start your work life in the U.S.

Key Steps to Life in the U.S. After You Land That Job

Social Security Number

I talked about getting a social security number (SSN) above, but this is such an important part of American life that it deserves more attention. This number is key to how you will function in the U.S. system. Once you have been assigned an SSN you will have it for life so if you applied for and received an SSN on a previous visa, like a J1, you do not have to file for one again.

Your social security number, as stated above, is utilized for almost everything from getting credit cards, to buying a mobile phone, to signing a lease and to getting paid. Unfortunately most companies and people are under the wrong impression that you must have an SSN to get paid. That **is NOT entirely true**. You must have

APPLIED for an SSN. If you have applied for one your employer may enter the word APPLIED where they would normally write in your SSN on the employer tax forms. They can then update this information once you receive your SSN. If you tell an employer this and they do not believe you point them to this government site for confirmation. http://www.ssa.gov/pubs/10181.html#need

You can apply for a social security number a few days after you arrive in the U.S. on a work visa such as the H1B, the E3 or the J1. You should wait a few days to allow your arrival to register in the U.S. government system. You will need your passport with your visa, your I-94 card, a filled out application form and letter of employment. That's it. The card will be mailed to you in two to eight weeks, but you can go back to the same office a few days after you apply and ask them to tell you your number even if you have not received your SSN card in the mail.

Since this number is used for just about everything in the U.S. it is the basis for identity fraud in the U.S. Do not give this number out to anyone.

Healthcare and Health Insurance

The U.S. system of healthcare and health insurance is unlike any other system in the world. The first thing to know about U.S. healthcare is that there is no public health system in the U.S. The U.S. system is firstly a for-profit business and secondarily a way to care for people. It is extremely expensive and there is virtually no safety net. If you are used to your government covering half, most or all of your health and medication costs you will need to adapt as the U.S. government will not pay for healthcare costs. If you had private insurance in your country the monthly premiums, while seeming excessive to you, will pale in comparison to the hundreds of dollars a month required in the U.S. for basic coverage.

In most cases your employer will provide health insurance in four parts: medical, dental, prescription and optical. They will negotiate a "group" rate with the insurance company so the cost is somewhat less. That being said you will still be responsible for paying some of the insurance premium which typically amounts to $300-$400 per month. That amount can vary widely though so make sure you know what the cost will be. If your employer does not provide health insurance you can buy your own individual policy, but that will be even more expensive.

If you do not have private health insurance you will bear the cost for all of your medical expenses. Should you choose to see a doctor for a general check up at the casual rate you may end up owing hundreds of dollars in medical bills.

You should also be aware that although you have private health insurance your insurance company may not cover all medical expenses. Remember that they are a business just like any other. You can write letters to appeal an insurer's judgment about denying a healthcare claim though and many times will be able to get them to pay.

There are some terms that you should learn in order to understand your health insurance policy.

1. Deductible- this is a dollar amount that you must spend out of pocket on your medical care before your insurance will begin paying any of your costs. This amount can vary from $100 to several thousand dollars depending on the plan. Some plans have no deductible and begin paying the moment you visit a healthcare provider.
2. Co-pay- This is a payment made by you as a portion of your medical visit. It is generally $10-$50 depending on the plan. Some plans have no co-pay.
3. Rx: This is the U.S. abbreviation for prescription.
4. In-network- Health insurance providers negotiate with doctors for lower rates so that the plan will cover all or most of the cost for visits to these specific doctors.
5. Out-of-Network- Providers that are not in the plan's network will cost you more. Some plans cover 80-90% of the costs for out-of-network providers while others provide no coverage at all if you use an out-of-network doctor.

The Current Healthcare Debate in America

There is a huge debate occurring in the U.S. right now about the healthcare system. There is some consensus that changes are needed to make healthcare more affordable in general, but how to go about achieving that goal is heatedly debated.

To provide some additional background on the current system here are some pros and cons of the current U.S. system.

Pros
- The U.S. has some of the best medical facilities and access to the widest range of highly skilled doctors and specialists in the world.
- Extremely convenient access to numerous pharmacies and medical locales for the majority of the population.
- For those with good health insurance there is generally a very high standard of care.
- For most people with health insurance (about 80% of the U.S. population) the vast majority of the costs are covered by their employer.
- There is a government run Medicare program that covers the majority of healthcare costs for senior citizens.
- There is a government run Medicaid program run by each individual state that helps to cover costs for impoverished citizens.

Cons
- The U.S. is the only rich, industrialized nation in the world that does not have universal health coverage for all citizens.
- Close to 50 million citizens have no health insurance and many more are under-insured, meaning they do not have enough coverage.
- The U.S. government spends more on health care per citizen than any nation in the world, but not all citizens are covered.
- The costs for employers and individuals are out of control which incurs flow on effects to everything from much

higher domestic flight costs on U.S. airlines to the largest cause of foreclosures and bankruptcies for individuals.
- It is very much a disease care system which, in my opinion, causes a huge over prescription of medications.
- The entire system is profit based which may provide an incentive to keep people on medication and to deny them coverage.
- The U.S. lags many nations (both rich and poor) in key healthcare indicators such as infant mortality rate, overall health rating, etc.
- There are concepts like 'Pre-Existing Conditions' whereby insurance companies will deny your coverage because you had this or a related condition prior to starting your plan with them.

With those pros and cons laid out let's get more into the actual debate. There are essentially two issues that are being debated in Congress, across the country and in the media. They are:

1. How to control healthcare costs
2. How to make healthcare affordable to all citizens

Now, most of the country is on board with wanting to reach both of these goals. The issue is exactly how to achieve them. The left generally wants a Universal Healthcare system provided by the U.S. government. The right wants a combination of tax credits and refunds so that people can buy insurance themselves. The right is also arguing for some legal reforms to tame the crazy amount of litigation that surrounds healthcare.

The biggest impediment in the debate though is that both sides (Democrat and Republican) receive lots of campaign contributions from the healthcare industry which clearly affects their positions. Also, with much of Congress being drawn from the legal profession, legal reforms tend to not be a popular issue to tackle.

Healthcare and Immigration

So how will the healthcare debate affect immigrants? For the most part nothing will change for illegal immigrants and legal immigrants on work visas. The Universal Healthcare plans are probably going to be available to only U.S. citizens and permanent residents. You will still need to rely on employer provided insurance or a policy you have purchased yourself.

While this debate continues it is still illegal for any U.S. hospital to turn away someone who comes in for treatment. This fact clogs up emergency rooms and actually adds flow on costs to everyone via higher taxes and insurance costs.

Exactly how this debate will end and how the U.S. healthcare system will change, if at all, is still anyone's guess. My best advice is to learn the system and know how to talk with doctors and your insurance company so that you can get the healthcare you deserve at a reasonable cost to you.

Taxes

Taxes in the U.S. will depend on what type of visa you are on. The details of taxes per visa will be covered in later chapters, but suffice it to say that the U.S. tax structure is complicated. Depending on your visa type you will have to contend with Federal, State, Medicare and Social Security taxes.

I know that was a lot of information to absorb about the U.S. job search and life in the United States in general. You may want to read this chapter several times to take it all in and may wish to do extra research on topics like healthcare. Since this book is about immigration, not healthcare, the information given here is just the tip of the iceberg.

The next four chapters will be devoted to specific visa types. Life in the United States, and especially the healthcare system, works the same no matter which one of these visas you are on.

Chapter 4: J1 Visa

The J1 visa is a non-immigrant visa that allows foreign nationals to enter the U.S. in order to hold internships or participate in scholarly exchange programs to promote the sharing of knowledge and skills. The J1 visa is actually extremely flexible and can be a great way to travel and work in the U.S. In fact many people utilize the J1 visa as a way to prelude life in the U.S. before moving on to a full working visa such as the H1B or E3. Compared to the H1B visa the J1 is a piece of cake.

There are two separate types of J1 visas that although they have similar requirements are still quite distinct from each other. These two distinct types are:

1. The Internship (INT) or Professional Career Training (PCT) Programs,
2. The Work and Travel Program (WAT).

Let's walk through each visa type so that you will understand how each works and can then determine which one is right for your situation.

Internship (INT) and Professional Career Training (PCT) Programs

The J1's INT and PCT Programs are part of a broad group of programs referred to as 'Trainee' programs. The types of people/positions that tend to be sponsored under these programs are:

- Medical trainees
- Veterinary trainees
- Pharmaceutical trainees
- Aviation trainees
- Academic/Research trainees

These categories are some of the typical positions that are sponsored, but you can be sponsored for many types of roles under the J1 visa. It is not limited to specific fields.

The basic regulations of the INT Program are as follows:

- The candidate must be enrolled on a full-time basis at a nationally accredited tertiary institution like a college or university, but they can start their role up to 6 months after their graduation.
- The person must be at least 18 years old.
- The person must have sufficient English language ability to function normally in a business setting.
- The candidate must be at least one year into their chosen field of study and the end result of their study must result in a degree, certificate, qualification, etc. such as a bachelor's degree.
- The trainee program should have correlation with the candidate's course of study (this is loosely applied given that most roles have very vague job descriptions).
- You can obtain visas via the INT program multiple times; however, it has to be shown that the new program is not a duplicate of a previous program
- Dependents may come and work in the U.S. on a partner visa called the J2. (A nice little perk!)

There are some differences between the regulations of the INT Program and the PCT Program so let's walk through the basic regulations of the PCT Program.

- The trainee has to be a graduate of a tertiary institution with at least 1 year of non-U.S. work experience related to their qualifications OR have at least 5 years work experience.
- The trainee must be a high school graduate.
- The trainee should be between 20 and 40 years of age.

- Like the INT program, the person must have sufficient English language ability to function normally in a business setting.
- Also similar to the INT program, if this is a subsequent PCT program it has to be shown it is not duplicative of previous training or work experience
- Since 2007, a 2 year 'Home Residency Requirement' (HRR) applies to all countries, meaning that after the PCT Program the candidate must remain outside the U.S. for at least two years. He/She is not allowed to return on a work visa, although a tourist visa may be approved.
- This 2 year residency rule may be waived under certain circumstances, but the process can be long and drawn out.
- Dependents may come and work in the U.S. on a partner J2 visa as well.

Before we go into the details of the J1 WAT program let's explain more about the HRR, or 2 year residency rule, and the possibility of getting a waiver for this rule. This rule applies to the PCT Programs only. The PCT Program is meant to foster knowledge sharing by having the foreign national return to their home country to share their knowledge after their training in the U.S. There are a lot of reasons though that might preclude a visitor from returning to their home country. For these situations there is a waiver provision which is solely at the discretion of the United States government. It should be noted that the process for this waiver is generally long and drawn out and it is a good idea to start early. The U.S. government is not known for its speed. Also, the waiver is not for those that just like working in the U.S. and wish to stay for a while longer.

The following categories may be deemed appropriate for a waiver.

1. Medical students who entered in to the United States during school and now post graduation they would like to stay back in the United States.
2. People who are foreign nationals and came to the United States in order to participate in a government funded program. The same would also apply to other programs in

the U.S. that are funded by other countries or by other international organizations.

3. Foreign nationals, who attended the exchange program and are now required to go back to their home country, but whose knowledge would be of little or no importance back home due to the lack of resources in their home country.

4. If the J1 visa holder is able to obtain an NOC, or a no objection certificate, from the government in his home country.

5. If the project the J1 visa holder is working on is of importance to the federal government or any of its agencies, the federal government might choose to waive the restriction.

6. If by complying with the J1 visa clause it would be subjecting the spouse and the children of the person to a lot of hardship and problem the case may be reviewed for a waiver. But under such a situation the children and the spouse of the person have to be citizens or at least permanent residents of the United States.

Here are the steps you need to take to apply for the 2 year HRR waiver.

1. Complete the online J1 Visa Waiver Recommendation Application, DS-3035. This form must be completed online. You cannot submit this form in any other way. It must be submitted online. Once the form is submitted your information will be downloaded into a barcode and you will receive a waiver case number and further instructions. You now need to print this online DS-3035 form with the barcode. The barcode must be printed in black and white only.

2. Mail your waiver application and processing fee to the U.S. State Department. Include the following in this mailing:

   - Your Form DS-3035 with barcode
   - Legible copies of every/all Form DS-2019/IAP-66 ever issued to you
   - Two self-addressed, stamped legal-size envelopes
   - The application fee- $215 U.S.D

If using the U.S. Postal Service mail the package to:

U.S. Department of State
Waiver Review Division
P.O. Box 952137
St. Louis, MO 63195-2137

If using a Courier Service send the package to:

U.S. Department of State
Waiver Review Division
(Box 952137)
1005 Convention Plaza
St. Louis, MO 63101-1200

3. Submit Supporting Documents (or have them submitted on your behalf) - The exact supporting documents submitted will depend on your reason for applying for the waiver. The document(s) should be one of the following listed here:

- No Objection Statement
- Request by an Interested U.S. Federal Government Agency
- A letter detailing the persecution you would face should you return home
- A letter detailing the Exceptional Hardship to a U.S. Citizen (or lawful permanent resident) spouse or child that will occur should you be forced to leave the U.S.
- Request by a Designated State Public Health Department or its Equivalent (Conrad State 30 Program)

It is your responsibility to make sure these documents are sent to the Waiver Review Division at the address below.

U.S. Department of State
Visa Services
Waiver Review Division
2401 E Street, NW
Washington, DC 20522-0106

4. Check your Waiver Request Status and Update your Contact Information. Use the following website to check your status and ensure that all supporting documents have been received. (https://j1visawaiverrecommendation.state.gov/) You can also use this website to check if your waiver has been approved. Simply enter your case number and select "Check Your Status". If your contact information changes for any reason while waiting for the waiver process to complete use this website as well to update your information.

5. If the Waiver Review Division needs more information from you they will contact you via the information in the system and ask for the additional documents or information. If you need to send additional documents mail them to this address.

U.S. Department of State
Visa Services
Waiver Review Division
2401 E Street, NW
Washington, DC 20522-0106

6. Application processing- This process varies greatly depending on why you are applying for a waiver. It can take from 4 to 8 weeks if your waiver is requested by a U.S. Government Agency all the way up to 3 to 4 months if you are applying due to a hardship or persecution. The best advice is to stay patient and to continue to check on your status.

7. Department of State Recommendation and Final Determination by the USCIS- In this step you will learn if the State Department has recommended that your waiver be granted. Their recommendation is then sent to the USCIS which will make the final determination in your case. You

will be notified directly at the address listed in the system. Good luck!

Since we've covered the details of the INT and PCT programs plus the HRR waiver rules and process, let's compare the INT and PCT programs to the J1 Work and Travel (WAT) Program.

J1 WAT Program

The WAT program is often known as a "cultural exchange" visa and is designed for current high school, college or university students to visit and work in the U.S. during their long holidays like summer break. It is considered the "fun" visa by many foreign students. The length of the visa is for up to 4 months. (Australian and New Zealand citizens now have access to a special 12 month WAT program. It works in the same manner as the general WAT program, just for a longer period of time.) The exact length of the visa is determined by a combination of how long their program is and how long their school break is. In the end though the visa's length is up to the local U.S. Consulate and what they are willing to grant based on the two earlier factors and what country the applicant is from.

Unlike the INT and PCT programs the WAT program does not generally grant a J2 visa for dependents. For the most part, this makes sense as the majority of those applying for the WAT program are students and do not have any dependents.

Some usual purposes for the J1 WAT visa are:

- High School Exchange Programs
- Work and Travel for college students
- Au Pair
- Camp U.S.A programs
- YMCA camp counselors
- Some government and academic programs.

The J1 WAT program is truly made for students to come over and work for a short time and do some traveling before or after their work assignment. The idea is to help foster cross cultural learning and friendship both for the foreign nationals and U.S. students as well.

How to Find a Job for the J1 Visa

Before we get into how exactly to find a job for your J1 visa there are a few things associated with this visa that need to be understood. First, the company that employs you is called your "host" company, not your sponsor or employer. Second, on the J1 visa there will be a "middleman" organization that will server as your official sponsor and can help you with finding a job if you wish.

Finding a job position that will allow you to come to the U.S. on a J1 visa can seem daunting at first if you do not have many U.S. contacts. There are several ways that most people are able to find their J1 job. Many use the organizations that will eventually sponsor them to help with the job search. Each of these companies has their own Internet Job Search Engine so make sure to check them out online. Here are 3 of the best sponsor companies.

1. Intrax
2. InterExchange
3. CIEE

More sponsor companies do exist, these are just considered some of the best and it's always good to start with the best.

If you utilize these companies your first point of contact will be someone at these companies who will screen you for positions before they present you to the employer or "host". These interviews are done so that the sponsor company can pass along the best candidates to the employer for each position. Additionally, there are always fees owed to the sponsor organization for finding the job for you. If you find an internship yourself, which is allowed, and use the sponsor organization only to sponsor you these additional fees will not be charged.

Whether or not these companies actually find your internship they will sponsor your J1 visa. If you find your internship on your own both you and your host company will need to fill out application forms on the sponsor's website and they will then contact you about processing the application. Of course, you will have to pay a program fee as well as almost nothing about the U.S. immigration system is free.

If you decide to search for a job on your own here is a listing of many websites that can help with internship roles.

- Internjobs.com
- Indeed.com
- Craigslist.org
- Truecareers.com
- Interships4you.com
- Nationjob.com
- Simplyhired.com
- Juju.com
- Job-hunt.org
- Experience .com
- JobbankU.S.a.com
- Job.com
- Careerjet.com
- Careersite.com
- Jobvillage.com
- Internweb.com

Unlike the more long term full work visas, there are many companies that are willing to hire you without a face to face interview. They will often extend a job offer based on a phone interview or even video chat via Skype. Most of these companies have hired foreign interns before.

Be aware that well paid internships are hard to find. Most internships are either unpaid or pay a very minimal stipend. If you are comfortable with minimal pay you will also need to prove before your J1 is approved that you have sufficient funds to support yourself while in the U.S.

The higher paid internships are hard to find because there are many U.S. citizens interested in these roles and many of the employers interested in foreign interns are looking for cheap labor. You can, however, negotiate your pay and don't be afraid to ask your employer for more money before you agree to the internship's terms. You can offer to have them pay you as a contractor rather than an official employee, thereby allowing them to avoid U.S. payroll taxes, but understand that this arrangement will have tax implications for you. You will be responsible for paying the payroll taxes that the employer generally pays to the IRS and believe me that you do not want to play games with the IRS as they can drastically effect your immigration or permanent resident application in the future.

Don't forget that you will also have to file taxes in the U.S. after December 31st of the year in which you worked in the U.S. Generally filing your taxes under the J1 visa is easy and you will typically get money back from the U.S. government as you will have earned less than the minimum salary to owe taxes. You can file your taxes online and the U.S. Government will mail you a check in USD to your home country or they can deposit the money into your U.S. bank account.

There are many ways to find an internship position in the U.S. Plan on the application process with the sponsor organization taking 1-2 months on average, so start looking for a position well in advance.

After your sponsor has approved your position and filed the proper paperwork they will give you a DS-2019 Form which shows that they have approved your position. You will need to take this form with your visa application to the U.S. Consulate for your J1 visa interview. Once your interview is complete, assuming your visa was approved, you should be able to book your travel to the U.S. and start your new internship.

J1 Visa Costs

The costs for the J1 visa are straightforward, but not incredibly small even though this is a fairly simple and generally short term visa. It is rather amazing the fees surrounding this visa when many of the internships are so poorly paid.

The first fee is the Program Fees which are paid to your sponsor organization. The exact amount is calculated based on how many months your program is with about $1500 being the amount for a full 18 month program. This fee will often include the cost for mandatory health insurance, but not always so make sure to ask.

If health insurance coverage is not included in the Program Fees you will have to buy your own insurance. Your sponsor company should be able to give you a list of approved providers. If they can't give you this list and don't cover the cost in their Program Fees look for a different sponsor.

The next fee is the SEVIS Fee which stands for Student Exchange Visitor Information System. SEVIS is a computer system that was instituted after September 11, 2001 to track high school, work and travel, trainee and other student/cultural visa holders. The SEVIS fee is currently $200, but is waived for some government sponsored cultural positions.

The last set of fees is the fees for the U.S. Consulate/Embassy Application. These fees will vary depending on your home country and city. It is best to check with the U.S. Consulate in your area to assess what their fees will be.

The J1 visa is a great way to come to the U.S., make some money and get a foothold to launch your full time job search. If your plan is to stay for the long term and transfer to a more permanent work visa just make sure you go through the right program. If you utilize the PCT program you will have a 2 year restriction on your working in the U.S. unless you go through the cumbersome waiver process. It is much easier to start the J1 on the INT program and transfer from there.

If your plan is more to come to the U.S., have a temporary job and then do some traveling then the WAT program is perfect for you. You can come, work for a few months and then spend a few weeks traveling around the country. There are so many amazing places to see in the U.S. so you can easily spend one or two weeks touring the country. Just make sure to budget based on where you are going and how you want to travel. Please take note that unlike Europe, Asia and other parts of the world there are no real discount airlines and car rentals tend to be more expensive in the U.S. summer months than at other times of the year. Whatever you decide enjoy your time in the U.S.

Chapter 5: H1B Visa

The H1B Visa is a non-immigrant visa classification used by professionals that want to work in the U.S. in various occupations including accounting, engineering, architecture, law, medicine, computing, teaching, social work and other areas. Those who apply for this visa must hold a bachelor's degree or equivalent credentials. Their educational credentials will be evaluated if they hold a foreign degree.

The United States Customs and Immigration Service (USCIS) will evaluate the credentials and decide if the degree or experience meets the minimum requirements to obtain an H1B visa. If your degree is from a foreign university, or you do not have a bachelor's degree, you are required to demonstrate that your education and/or experience are equal to a U.S. bachelor's degree. Demonstrating your credentials will include completing a college-level equivalency test (such as CLEP) or an assessment by a recognized service specializing in the evaluation of foreign country educational credits.

H1B Process

Now let's get into how the H1B process works. The first thing to note is that there is an annual quota for H1B visas. The quota is currently set at 65,000 per year. There is also an additional quota of 20,000 visas for foreign nationals who hold a master's degree or higher from a U.S. institution. Please note that once that 20,000 quota is filled any remaining candidates with higher degrees will be rolled into the group vying for one of the 65,000 quota spots. Thus anyone with a higher degree from a U.S. institution essentially has two shots at an H1B visa. There are also some special quotas under Free Trade Agreements for Chilean and Singaporean citizens which total 6,800. These visas do not currently take away from the overall 65,000 quota and they have to date never reached the full limit in any one year. Plus any of the unused visas for Chilean or Singaporean citizens from the current year are added to the following year's available quota. Also, any non-immigrants who work at (but not necessarily for) universities or non-profit research facilities do not count towards the cap. This exclusion includes contractors as well as employees.

So how is it determined which candidates get one of the 65,000 visas? Well, that question requires some background to truly answer. Back in FY2001, FY2002, and FY2003 the quota limit was temporarily raised to 195,000 visas per year for numerous reasons including the large number of foreign nationals that wished to come to the U.S. to work and the demand of U.S. companies for their talents. In FY2004 though the quota was lowered to 65,000 and it has remained at that level ever since.

In years such as 2006-2008 there were significantly more applicants than there were visas available. To determine who would receive a visa and who wouldn't a lottery system was devised. Each year on April 1, candidates can file applications with the USCIS. Assuming you are granted a visa in the lottery, the first day you are eligible to work for your employer under their new H1B status is October 1. As a side note, during the years before the recession it was not unusual for the USCIS to receive over 100,000 applications on the first day.

The last few years has seen a sharp decline in the number of H1B visa applications filed with some years the 65,000 quota not being reached until the next calendar year. This fact is probably due to the high unemployment in the U.S. meaning that fewer jobs are available as a whole and for foreign nationals in particular.

H1B Application Tips

If you are applying for an H1B visa here are some tips for getting your application approved, especially when the demand for visas goes back up to the pre-recession levels.

1. Ensure that all of your documentation is submitted with your petition. Don't provide some documentation thinking that you will submit more later. That approach will probably get your application rejected or at least delayed significantly.

2. Submit your petition in a timely manner. When there were far more applications than visas available this tip meant that you should have your application submitted on April 1. (The USCIS did tend to close application submission after only a few days when the volume was extremely high.)
3. Ensure that your petition is sent to the proper USCIS adjudication center for your region. If it is sent to the incorrect center it can be denied or bounced around the system for far too long.
4. H1B status is most often reached by people studying on the F1 visa, working under the F1 visa OPT (Occupational Practical Training) periods or working under a J1 visa.

Required Documentation

Now that we've discussed some general tips let's get into the specific documents you will have to file for your H1B visa petition. As noted above make sure you have all these documents together and that they are submitted with your application. Don't submit the application first and think you can submit the other documents later. Here is a list of documents from the USCIS you will have to provide.

- Form I-907 (if filing for Premium Processing Service)
- Form G-28 (if represented by an attorney or accredited representative)
- Form I-129, Petition for a Nonimmigrant Worker
- H Classification Supplement to Form I-129
- H-1B Data Collection and Filing Fee Exemption Supplement
- All supporting documentation to establish eligibility
  - Arrival-Departure Record (Form I-94) if the beneficiary is in the U.S.
  - SEVIS Form I-20 if the beneficiary is a current or former F-1 student or F-2 dependent
  - SEVIS Form DS-2019 if the beneficiary is a current or former J-1 or J-2

- o   Form I-566 if the beneficiary is a current A or G nonimmigrant
- o   Department of Labor certified LCA, Form ETA 9035
- o   Employer/attorney/representative letter(s); and
- o   Other supporting documentation. (See below for further detail.)

Other Supporting Documentation

When filing for an H1B visa you will need supporting documentation from both the beneficiary (the worker) and the petitioner (the employer). Below is a list of typical documents that both parties may submit. All of these documents are not necessary, but it is always better to err on the side of sending too much supporting documentation.

The supporting documentation from the beneficiary is meant to prove that he/she meets the H1B visa eligibility criteria. The typical additional supporting documents filed by the beneficiary are as follows:

- Educational information such as post-secondary degrees and transcripts
- Work experience letters, if necessary
- Educational and/or work experience evaluations or letters, as necessary
- A copy of the applicant's passport and other biographical information
- Copies of any relevant licenses, certifications, memberships or other pertinent documents

This information is critical because it proves to the USCIS that the beneficiary meets the H1B visa requirements and that he/she has the skills and ability for the position stated in the H1B application. Some of the documentation may not be necessary, but these are the types of documents you should be thinking about when applying. Essentially you want to provide ample evidence of your education and ability as it pertains to the position you are hoping to fill at your new employer.

If you currently reside in the U.S. it is important to provide documentation that you are maintaining your status. Documentation such as an I-94, pay stubs, I-20 forms, etc. can prove to the USCIS that you are here legally. Remember that if there is any doubt in their minds as to your status your application may be denied.

Supporting documentation from the petitioner (employer) is meant to prove that the employer is a legitimate company and that the beneficiary is going to work in the capacity outlined in the application. They need to prove that someone of the beneficiary's caliber is truly needed to fill the role. It is just as important for the employer to provide supporting documentation. Some common documents that the employer should provide are:

- Copy of the first page of the employer's most recent federal tax return
- Employer's articles of incorporation, if relevant
- Employer's annual report, any marketing material used by the employer, or the employer's corporate brochure as applicable.
- Printouts from the employer's website
- Printouts of any online references to the employer's work or projects.
- Any documentation that may be relevant to the beneficiary's proposed work position.

Due to the current political climate in the U.S. surrounding immigration there is a heightened level of scrutiny surrounding visa applications. Be aware that this fact has increased requests for evidence (RFE), notices of intent to deny (NOID) and flat out application denials. Be prepared for extra scrutiny around your application for an H1B visa.

Renewals, Extensions and Changing Employers

As we delve into the topics of renewing and/or extending your visa and changing employers let's first discuss the difference between H1B status and an H1B visa. Getting H1B status means that you are authorized to work in the U.S. H1B status is often granted to foreign nationals who are already working in the U.S. legally. Getting your H1B visa stamped means that you are authorized to enter and leave the U.S. so you have the ability to travel. If you are on H1B status and leave the U.S. for travel you will have to apply for your visa stamp at a consulate abroad.

Once you are granted your H1B it is good for a period of 3 years and is able to be renewed once for an additional 3 years giving you a maximum of 6 years. With new legislation passed in 2000 you can get a 1 year extension of your H1B past the six year limit if a labor certification has been pending for 365 days or longer whether or not a permanent residency or green card application has been filed.

An extension of your H1B is actually the extension of your authorization to travel. This term is not used to mean that you have a longer amount of time, but rather that you can travel freely in the U.S. and abroad. Basically if your visa is renewed you still need to have it stamped against the new extension in order to travel. This process is known as H1B revalidation. So basically if your visa is renewed beyond the 3 year period you will need to get your visa stamped at an overseas consulate or embassy if you are travelling abroad.

To change employers while on an H1B visa you need to have your new employer file a new Form ETA 9035 Labor Condition Application (LCA) and Form I-129. Please note that this petition must be filed before your last day of employment by your current employer. If it is filed after this date, you will be considered out of status and unable to change employers on your current H1B visa. If changing employers you will also have to prove that you have recent pay stubs (at least 60 days old) and last year's W2 forms, if applicable. If you do not have recent pay stubs you will need to be able to explain this situation to the USCIS. They do accept leave of absence and approved long term sick leave as potential exceptions.

A merger or sale of your sponsoring company does not necessarily change your visa status and you may need to do nothing. If however you are performing duties that differ from what is stated on your H1B application then this can be considered a visa violation.

If you are laid off and the USCIS is notified you will be considered immediately out of status and can be asked to leave the country immediately.

H1B Visa Costs

One key thing to note when thinking about applying for an H1B visa is the cost. If you're lucky your employer will pick up all the costs or at least most, but if you are paying for the entire process the dollars can quickly add up. Here are the key costs and fees associated with the H1B visa. Keep in mind that if you use a lawyer there will be additional legal costs on top of the costs listed here.

1. USCIS filing fee with USCIS- $325- Form I-129 (Spouse optional H4 fee is $300)
2. Fraud Detection fee paid to USCIS- $500
3. LCA Filing Fee with Department of Labor- FREE – Form ETA 9035/9035e
4. Premium Filing Fee- $1225- this is an optional service that is designed to help the process by allowing your legal representative access to your case officer's phone number and decisions pertaining to your application are to be made within 15 days. It can also aid your spouse's H4 visa process, if applicable.
5. ACWIA Fee- $750 or $1500 – This fee is paid if your petition is successful. It goes towards training for U.S. Workers. It is $1500 unless your employer has fewer than 25 fulltime employees. Some government, education and non-profit institutions are exempt from this fee.
6. Consular Application Fee - $131 (an additional $131 for your spouse)

So as you can see by these numbers the costs do add up very quickly. If you add in legal fees it can seem overwhelming. If you do hire a lawyer do your research and try to find a fixed cost for all legal processing.

Do I Need a Lawyer

The truth is that you do not need a lawyer to file for and obtain an H1B visa. With fewer applicants recently this may be even more true, but for an H1B visa it is something you should consider. The process and rules around this visa are very convoluted and in my opinion, intentionally so. If your employer is handling the whole process they will have attorneys to walk your application through the system.

If you are handling the process yourself please remember that large corporations, in particular, have lawyers that are doing everything they can to ensure that their candidates have the best chance of getting a visa, plus these companies are absolutely paying the Premium Filing Fee. While the number of applicants is staying beneath the 65,000 quota you may be able to handle the process without a lawyer, but you will need to do significant research on the full process. You can pay the Premium Filing Fee yourself, but I have yet to hear of the immigration officers talking to anyone other than lawyers. Again, if hiring a lawyer do your research and try to find one that will take your case on a fixed retainer.

How to Transfer to an H1B from Other Visas

Transferring from another visa to an H1B visa can be complicated and how the process works is dependent on the visa you are transferring from. Please note that a change in status is not automatically granted even if you qualify. The USCIS will also determine how long to extend your visa period based on your unique case. Sometimes it can all seem very arbitrary, but generally if USCIS deems your intentions are genuine and you have not violated your current status your petition will be successful. That being said you should note that there are some visas that you CANNOT transfer from while in the U.S. so you will have no choice but to leave and apply for a new visa.

The list of the visas that you cannot transfer from includes:

- C Visa (aliens in transit)
- D Visa (Usually for flight/ship staff, etc.)
- K1.K2 (fiancée visa and dependent of fiancée)
- S Visa (witness or informant)
- TWOV (transit without visa)
- Tourist under waiver program classified when you receive Green I-94W form when you enter the U.S.

Please also note:

- J1 visa- can't transfer/extend if they are subject to the 2 year residency rule, unless you have followed the proper (and long) government channels to get this condition revoked
- M1- They can't transfer to the H visa category where the training helped them qualify for the H visa

Besides having to be on a visa that allows you to transfer to an H1B visa there are some additional basic requirements that you must meet to change your status. These requirements are:

- You must have entered the U.S. legally
- You have not done anything in the U.S. to immediately disqualify yourself such as commit a crime
- There are no factors that require you to leave the U.S. prior to re-entry under your new status
- You have submitted your application prior to the expiration date recorded on your I-94 form given to you and stamped/dated when you entered the U.S.

To begin your transfer you must file form I-129 with the USCIS for the visa categories below. Approval for your change of status must be approved before you begin performing any activities under your new visa category. If you have a spouse and/or dependents they need to file form I-539 to change their status. If you have a spouse and/or dependents it is a good idea to file all at the same time so that they are judged at the same time. All dependents can be filed on the same I-539 form.

This is the list of visa categories requiring the I-129 form:

- **E1/E2** (Treaty Traders and Investors)

- **E3** (Australian temporary worker)

- **H1B/H2A/H2B/H3** (Temporary Workers)

- **L1A/L1B** (Intra-company Transferee)

- **O1/O2** (Aliens with Extraordinary Ability)

- **P1/P2/P3** (Athletes & Entertainers)

- **Q1** (International Cultural Exchange)

- **R1** (Religious Workers)

- **TN1/TN-2** (Canadians & Mexicans covered under the North American Free Trade Agreement (NAFTA))

For spouses and/or dependents to qualify for the visa categories below you have to file form I-539.

- **A** (Diplomatic & Other Government Officials, Immediate Family members, Employees)

- **B1/B2** (Visitors for Business or Pleasure)

- **E** (Treaty Traders & Investors Dependents Only)

- **F** (Academic Students & Dependents)

- **G** (Foreign Government Officials & Certain Immediate Family Members)

- **H4** (Temporary Worker Dependents Only)

- **K3/K4** (Spouse of U.S. Citizen & Minor Child Accompanying)

- **L2** (Intra-company Transferee Dependents Only)

- **M** (Vocational & Language Students and Dependents)

- **N** (Parents & Children of Certain People Who Have Been Granted Special   Immigrant Status)

- **NATO** (NATO Representatives, Officials, Employees, and Immediate Family Members)

- **O3** (Aliens with Extraordinary Ability Dependents Only)

- **P4** (Athletes and Entertainer Dependents Only)

- **R2** (Religious Worker Dependents Only)

- **TD** (TN Dependents Only)

The USCIS recommends that you file for your transfer about 60 days prior to your I-94 expiration date. You are allowed to remain in the U.S. while your transfer case is pending even if this is beyond you I-94 expiration date, but you will not be able to perform any activities, i.e. work or study, until your case is approved. For students there is actually an early initial approval you can receive to allow you to begin your studies at the start of a semester.

To check your case status you will be mailed a receipt with your case number on it. You can then enter this number on the USCIS website to see where your application is in the process. In general the whole process should not take more than a few weeks.

Transferring from the F1 Visa

As discussed in chapter 2, the F1 visa is a fulltime student visa and used mostly by international students from all over the world to study at U.S. colleges and universities. It is very popular and historically has been a way for foreign students to come to the U.S. and then transfer to the H1B visa. It is possible to transfer from the F1 to the H1B and there are four things the F1 lets you do that greatly enhance your chances of finding an employer to sponsor your H1B visa.

1. Curriculum Practical Training (CPT) – allows you to work for credits to your degree (don't do more than 12 months as it makes you ineligible for OPT).
2. Occupational Practical Training (OPT) – is one year for undergraduates and now possibly up to two years for master's or higher degree holders to work at a U.S. company. This program is usually done following graduation.
3. Network! – That's right network with your follow students, alumni, and others you meet in the above training programs. These contacts can help and support you both on transferring to an H1B and in so many other ways.
4. Time – Since you are already in the U.S. you will have so much more time to do things like build your resume, apply for jobs and attend interviews.

The F1 Visa is actually one of the easiest visas to transfer from to the H1B visa.

Top 10 H1B Visa Companies and H1B Cities for 2011

So what companies are hiring and sponsoring H1B applicants? Well, here is the list of the Top 10 H1B Visa Companies for 2011 ranked by their monthly Visa spend. These numbers come from Rediff and look at how much each company spends each month on H1B visa related issues.

Company	Monthly Spend
Microsoft	$226,901
Patni Americas	$67,744
Oracle	$61,592
Satyam	$60,032
Fujitsu	$51,682
Cognizant	$38,857
Polaris	$38,354

Marlabs	$32,233
Larsen & Toubro Infotech	$31,550
Tata	$30,930

As you can see this list is dominated by high tech and bio tech companies. They are obviously seeking highly skilled foreign engineers, computer scientists and graduate level foreign workers. Many of these workers will probably have graduated as students on F1 visas from top American universities.

Here is the list of Top 10 H1B Cities in 2011 ranked by the monthly spend on H1B visa related issues by companies in these cites.

City	Monthly Spend
New York	$112,335
Mountain View	$90,529
Cupertino	$88,143
Palo Alto	$87,832
Redmond	$87,086
Santa Clara	$85,032
Sunnyvale	$81,028
Chicago	$78,312
San Jose	$77,273
San Francisco	$72,442

It should be no surprise that the top 10 cities list in many ways matches the list of the top 10 companies. Seven of the ten cities in this list are in the Bay Area and Silicon Valley in California home to the U.S. tech industry. Plus, Redmond is home to Microsoft and New York and Chicago both have large technology, finance, health and other industries that draw talent.

Opinions of the H1B Visa Process

I know that this chapter is very heavy on facts and lists. All of these lists are important to help you understand the H1B visa and the process. In closing though I want to discuss some of my opinions on the H1B process and why I think it is overall unfair.

1. The visa application cost is just frankly extremely high. If you have to pay all the fees yourself it is a very large cost to bear. Plus, if your application is denied only some of the fees are refundable.
2. The Premium Processing Fee- Although this extra fee is not supposed to "help" your application all the big companies pay it in order to ensure that everything is correct with their applications. The big companies get their applications approved at a higher rate.
3. Visa Lottery- Once employment increases again in the U.S. the cap of 65,000 will be way too limited and a ridiculously arbitrary limit to set. So many companies need the specialized talent that many foreigners have so for the U.S. government to set such a low cap is not helping anybody in the U.S. economy.
4. Lawyers- The system is so convoluted that the only people that win are the immigration lawyers and I am sure they are lobbying to keep it that way!
5. Lack of Incentive for Permanent Residency/Green Card- Coming to the U.S., paying your taxes and working hard is not the easiest way to gain residency status. Some applicants have to stay in their current role, turn down promotions and salary increases while waiting 10 years or more to become permanent residents.
6. Tax Burden- Immigrants must pay the same taxes that U.S. citizens do, but they are not entitled to benefits like Social Security or Medicare. In other words, they must pay into the system, but they cannot benefit from it.
7. Hire Dates- If you submit your application on April 1 and it is approved you still cannot start work for your employer under you H1B status until October 1. It does not make sense to keep someone who is approved from working for such a long period of time.

In closing this chapter I hope the information here has helped you understand how to navigate the H1B visa process better and hopefully avoid some common mistakes. Remember to research and learn the U.S. immigration rules as best as you can. It can only help you navigate this labyrinth of a system.

Chapter 6: E3 Visa

The E3 Visa is a non-immigrant visa exclusively for Australian citizens allowing them to work in the U.S. It was created in 2005 after the Australia and United States Free Trade Agreement (AUSFTA) negotiated between the Howard Government in Australia and the Bush Administration in the U.S. It is not actually part of the agreement, but was created subsequent to it as a direct result of the trade agreement. It is essentially a visa that allows Australian citizens to work in the U.S. for 2 year rolling periods, mainly in professional roles.

The key provisions of this visa are as follows:

- You must have a bachelor's degree or equivalent work experience and/or certifications.
- You must have a job offer from a U.S. company prior to applying at the Consulate.
- You can NOT apply for a new E3 Visa from within the U.S.
- You must apply for the Visa from outside the U.S., but can go to the U.S. to look for a job. You just must leave before you actually apply for the visa.
- The E3 is for applicants seeking employment in a specialty occupation, one requiring a specialized body of knowledge.
- The visa is valid for 2 years and you are able to renew it indefinitely for subsequent 2 year periods as long as the job position is still valid and not considered permanent.
- You must show that you intend to return home when your visa expires.
- The quota for the E3 visa is currently 10,500 per year (this does not include extensions or spouses), but the quota has yet to be reached in any one fiscal year.
- You may change employers, but your new employer must lodge a new Labor Condition Application (LCA) within 10 days.

Now let's walk through the process and elaborate on some of the above provisions. First you need to find an employer that is willing to hire and sponsor you in the U.S. As suggested in the chapter on finding a job in the U.S., I recommend you come to the States to look for a job. You will then have to leave to apply for the E3 visa, but you are much more likely to find a job if you are in the U.S.

Explaining the E3 Visa to an Employer

While looking for a job there is a very good chance that the potential employer will have no idea what an E3 visa is so be prepared to educate them. One of the best ways to explain the E3 to employers is to mention that it is very much like the TN visa for Canadians. Let them know that there is no cost to the employer, it can be filed and granted very quickly, at anytime of the year, and that it can be renewed indefinitely. Many employers are used to the TN visa for Canadians so hopefully this comparison will put their minds at ease. If they are still wary of sponsoring you, but are sold on you as a candidate, point them to online government resources so that they can learn more about the process.

After you get that job offer you will need to work with your soon to be employer and have them file form ETA-9035(e) with the U.S. Department of Labor. This form is filed so that your employer can receive an approved LCA. Filing the ETA-9035(e) is free and can be done online. The form essentially provides details on the nature of the job, the nature of the company, a little on the candidate and the salary. Please note that the salary has to meet Department of Labor standards for the average salary for your type of position and for that region of the country. (Cost of living can vary greatly within the U.S.)

Key Provisions of the E3 Visa

There are two key provisions of this visa that you must keep in mind while filing for the visa and also during your Consulate interview. First, is that your position must require a bachelor's degree as a minimum requirement for the job. You do not have to have a bachelor's degree if you can prove you have sufficient work experience. The point of the bachelor's degree is that the E3 is technically for "specialty occupations" which to the U.S. government means that you have to have specialized knowledge to execute the role well.

So allow me to digress for a little to provide more detail around what "sufficient work experience" means in terms of the E3 visa. The typical U.S. bachelor's degree takes 4 years to complete and it seems that 3 years of relevant work experience is counted towards 1 year of education. Therefore, the general rule of thumb is that you need 12 years of relevant work experience in order to prove educational equivalency. The key word in that sentence is RELEVANT. If you are applying for a job in high finance do not think that your work as a bartender or on a hotel courtesy desk will apply.

If you have relevant work experience and/or partial education the best way to prove that your experience and partial education meets the equivalency requirement is to have it accredited by a U.S. company or institution that specializes in these matters. If you don't have your experience accredited, then make sure to provide ample evidentiary documentation in your application and then again at your consular interview.

The types of evidentiary documents you should supply are: employer reference written on official letterhead, official company HR documents, any awards or certificates you received, any transcripts documenting the education you did complete and of course any other documents that prove either your educational status or your outstanding work experience. In this area it is much better to err on the side of having too much documentation.

After your application and documentation have been submitted you will be called for a consular interview. Remember that your visa is at the sole discretion of the U.S. consular officer assigned to your case. It will be up to that person's opinion as to whether or not your work experience meets the educational equivalency. Unfortunately it is often arbitrary and can seem cruel. If you are applying for a highly specialized occupation such as a bio-tech or nuclear role you are more likely to be approved even with less work experience as these roles are harder to fill by U.S. employers and immigrants with these skills are often in high demand. I know that makes the process even more arbitrary, but that's the way it is. You can try to fight the system, but it is highly unlikely that you will win. Now back to the key provisions of the E3 visa.

Dual Intent

You must also pay attention to the no dual intent clause of the visa regulations. So let's define dual intent. Dual intent is a condition of some non-immigrant visas in the U.S. that allows a person to pursue permanent status in the U.S. while on their current non-immigrant visa. Essentially, a candidate may be working toward a green card while they are in the U.S. on another type of visa. Be aware that the E3 does NOT allow for dual intent. The point is that you are supposed to be in the U.S. temporarily and then planning to return back home at the end of your visa.

To show that you do not have dual intent be prepared to demonstrate links to your home country. Do you have a residence there? Do you have extensive family back at home? Are all your bank accounts still in your home country? Remember to never lie on your application or during your Consulate interview, but at the same time talk about your ties back home and not about how you have so much family over in the U.S. and you can't wait to see them all. In other words, use some common sense!

The funny thing about the no dual intent part of this visa though is that the visa does not expressly forbid you from filing for permanent residency. In fact, you can file for permanent residency and still renew your E3 visa indefinitely. Yes, it's kind of strange.

U.S. Consulate Interview

After you receive your approved LCA you will need to schedule your interview with the U.S. Consulate. You can schedule your interview at any U.S. Consulate outside the United States and they will overall follow the same procedures, but there are some differences depending on the city/country so make sure to research the consulate you will be interviewed at for any differences.

Now assuming your interview is in Australia there are only 3 Consulate locations and they are in Melbourne, Sydney and Perth. If you are from a different section of the country you will have to travel for your interview.

To schedule your interview visit the VisaPoint site at https://aus.us-visaservices.com/Forms/default.aspx. It is best to schedule the appointment at least 4 weeks prior in order to get the date you ideally want as these fill up very quickly. It costs $14 AUD to schedule the interview and you have 90 days to login and reschedule this interview up to a maximum of 3 times. You have to schedule appointments for all passport holders who will be issued visas so if you have a spouse or kids you will need to pay $14AUD for each of them as well.

Here is an extensive list of items that you will need to bring to the interview as well.

1. The Labor Condition Application
2. A signed letter from the company (usually by HR or your department head) on official letterhead with job offer description addressed to you
3. The printed DS-160 online form confirmation page. The DS-160 is a form you have to complete online prior to attending the interview. You can complete this form anytime after you have scheduled your interview time and received your LCA confirmation number. This form details things like your personal information, recent world travels, complete work and education history as well as your planned U.S. itinerary and places you plan to stay. You can also upload a digital photo during this process. All of this is done in the VisaPoint system.
4. The printed VisaPoint interview time confirmation sheet (not usually necessary but doesn't hurt to have)

5. A self addressed envelope with postage paid (I generally recommend the Australia Post Express envelope which is about $4.50 and has a tracking code)
6. Confirmation receipt of application fee(s) paid for all visas at Australia Post (this has to be paid with a debit/atm card or cash NOT a credit card).
7. If you have Australian University degrees then bring a printed copy of these. (It doesn't hurt to have an academic transcript but is not usually asked for.)
8. Supporting documentation (this can include business titles, mortgage titles, bank account statements, etc. to show ties to Australia to demonstrate residence abroad)
9. If you don't have a University Degree and are proving that your experience, certifications and other qualifications are suitable for the E3 Visa Bachelor's Degree condition then you definitely need to bring evidence of all your work experience. Bring documented letters from former managers about your roles and tenure as well as transcripts and course descriptions for other qualifications. It can really help in these cases to get a U.S. based organization to do a degree/experience equivalency assessment that you can also present. This area is where additional Administrative Processing may be required and to avoid these long and ad hoc delays it is best to be over prepared.
10. Just in case take 2 additional U.S. sized (larger than Australian standard size) passport photos. Bring these in case the uploaded photo for your DS-160 online form is not deemed suitable. The U.S. consulate websites in Australia mention a couple of places nearby that do U.S. style passport photos.
11. Your Passport

The interview itself is in two parts. The first time you are called you will be handing over most of the documentation to your interviewer. He/She will collect your documents and may ask you a question or two. You will then be asked to sit down. The next time you are called it will be for your main interview. This is when you will be asked questions about your role, the company, your education, your experience, your dependents (if applicable) and possibly your ties to

Australia. Exactly how many questions you will be asked is dependent on your interviewer and your particular case.

People that get asked the most questions seem to be those without University degrees, those applying to positions that do not usually need a bachelor's degree, those applying to smaller, less well-known companies and those without extensive Australian ties.

You will also be required to give electronic fingerprints during this process so don't be surprised by this.

At the immediate conclusion of your main interview you will be told if your E3 visa is approved, denied or if administrative processing is needed. If your visa is approved and you provide your interviewer with an Express Post letter you will probably receive your passport 2-3 working days later in the mail. If denied you will get all of your documentation back immediately and be told the reason for your denial. If you are put in the administrative processing bucket you will be told what they are going to review in more detail and that they will be in touch. Unfortunately if you are put in administrative processing you are totally at the mercy of the system and it can take weeks or months. The worst part is that you will have no real way to find out anything meaningful about an estimated timeline or what is going on until they contact you. This can be very maddening!

Some people are put into the administrative processing bucket because they lied on their application and their lies are noticed or suspected by the U.S. consular officer. For these people their application will eventually be denied. In most cases though the "administrative processing" situation is more grey than that and is the result of the consular officer having hesitations due to some aspect of the application. The most common reasons for this are:

- He/She is unsure about the company as they have never sponsored an E3 visa before, are a small company or are not in a usual industry associated with this visa.
- He/She is unsure about the role as it sounds like a non-professional role or one which does not require a bachelor's degree.

- He/She is unsure about the candidate or something is amiss with their qualifications or experience and how it relates to the role or about their personal background from a security/character/criminal standpoint.
- He/She is unsure about the candidate's ties to Australia and if the candidate actually plans to return home.
- He/She is unsure about a dependent on the visa petition.

If this whole process sounds a little daunting, take a deep breath. For most people the entire E3 process goes smoothly, as long as you are prepared, and does not take very long to have an approved visa and be on your way to your new life in the U.S.

Working Part Time on the E3 Visa

One really nice thing about the E3 visa is that you are allowed to work part time for more than one employer as long as each role meets the visa criteria like being a Specialty Occupation. To accomplish this each employer has to be listed on your visa stamp in your passport with an approved LCA for each position. The minimum pay required also has to meet the criteria for the positions and for the city in which you are working.

E3 Partner Visa- the E3D

With the E3 visa there is a simple partner visa for dependents, the E3D. This visa is solely for dependents of Australians seeking an E3 visa, but the dependents do not have to be Australian citizens. The E3D visa does allow the holder to work in the U.S. providing they file form I-765 to the USCIS after entering the country. It customarily takes 2-3 months to receive the Employment Authorization Card (EAD) before the dependent can work. One thing to note is that the U.S. does not recognize defacto/common law couples or same sex couples. If your partner wants to come to the U.S. attached to your visa they must be married to you and usually an original marriage certificate is needed.

Do I Need a Lawyer to Get an E3 Visa?

One big question that comes up is do I need a lawyer to help me get an E3 visa. From the preceding pages in this chapter you can see that overall the process is very straightforward. For the most part I would recommend handling it on your own. I don't see the need to spend $2000 or more on a few forms and appointments that you need to schedule. With that being said many people will tell you that you need a lawyer due to issues centered around two topics:

1. The nature of the job and the salary
2. The no "dual intent" part of the visa.

Personally I think it is easy enough to handle these two issues yourself. There are some jobs that do not qualify for an E3 visa, but there are more than enough that do so you should be able to find a "professional" job that will meet the visa's criteria. As to dual intent, it's really pretty straightforward. Just make sure to establish some ties to your home country and it should not be a problem. Of course if you're still in doubt you can hire a lawyer to help walk you through the process.

E3 Renewal or Extension

If you are in the U.S. on an E3 visa it needs to be renewed every two years. You can either extend your current visa or apply for a new E3 visa. The difference is that an extension does not allow you to travel outside the U.S. while a new visa does; however, to receive a new E3 visa you must leave and re-enter the U.S. Many people take the route of getting a new visa by going to Canada as it is fairly close.

If you are merely extending your visa you can have your employer submit the ETA-9035 form as early as six months prior to your visa expiring. It is a good idea to submit this earlier rather than later as it can take the USCIS several months to process the paperwork. The USCIS will then send Form I-797 Approval Notice to your employer or the lawyer of record to notify you of their decision.

Differences between the E3 and H1B Visas

We've covered the basic differences between the E3 and H1B visas, but I wanted to provide a quick, bulleted list of these differences so that you can quickly understand these two visas in a nutshell.

1. The E3 visa is for Australian nationals only. The H1B visa is for citizens from any country in the world.
2. The E3 is renewable every 2 years indefinitely. The H1B visa is given for 3 years and can be renewed only once for an additional 3 year period.
3. The E3 visa has no government mandated application costs and requires only a free filing to the U.S. Department of Labor. The H1B has extensive filing and processing costs and requires a petition be submitted to the USCIS during a specified period of time.
4. The E3D Visa allows spouses to work in the U.S. There is no equivalent working visa for the H1B. The spouse of an H1B visa holder would need to also apply for a work visa in order to hold a job in the U.S.
5. The E3 visa is not specifically a dual intent visa whereas the H1B does allow for dual intent. That being said, the E3 does not expressly forbid filing for a green card while still working on the E3.
6. The H1B visa expressly states that the holder can start working at a new employer while their transfer application is pending. This provision is not explicitly stated in the E3 visa, but according the E3 rules when in doubt the E3 visa is supposed to follow the rules outlined in the H1B visa.

E3 Visa Contacts

If you have additional questions or specific questions about your visa application there are two information lines that you can call within Australia.

The first is a paid number- 1-902-941-641 which is charged $1.15 AUD per minute. This number has pre-recorded information that you can find on the U.S. Consulate website. This number is available 24 hours a day. You also have the option when you call this number to be connected to a live consultant who is available between 8:00am and 7:00pm Monday through Friday Australian Eastern Time. If you are connected to a live consultant the cost will be $3 per minute. If you need to call the consulate it is more helpful to speak to a live consultant so you can ask particular questions about more complex issues like administrative processing.

The second information line is a 1-800-687-844 number which is essentially the same live consultant service as the 1-902 number above, but without the pre-recorded information. The charge for this call is a flat $12 and can be charged to your credit card.

If you are thinking of calling either of these numbers please be aware that they never get specific on these lines about your personal details or application. They are more informational and procedural and they don't deviate from that so don't waste your money if your intention is to get details about your case.

In general your best option is really to read the U.S. Consulate website in detail and to study the E3 visa rules and regulations on the USCIS website as well.

That's the end of the detailed descriptions of non-immigrant visas. The next chapter will discuss immigrant visas (Green Cards) and the final chapter will walk you through the path to U.S. citizenship via the naturalization process.

Chapter 7: United States Green Card

The United States Green Card, or permanent residency, is a true immigrant visa that allows the bearer to remain in the U.S. indefinitely as long as he/she does nothing untoward that affects this status. The Green Card system was first started in the early 1800s as a National Defense program. With the huge influx of immigrants at that time the government created the system to help track them, which was an enormous task especially when you consider there were no computers at that time. Between 1820 and 1879 over 49 million immigrants came to the U.S. which helped the country grow by leaps and bounds. The system has grown and evolved over the years with over 1 million immigrant applications processed every year. One interesting thing to note is that the modern day Green Card is not actually green at all, in fact it appears that it was never green. Many people are often surprised by this fact when they see a Green Card for the first time.

What is a Green Card?

The Green Card itself is an identification card stating that the holder is entitled to permanent resident status in the U.S. The major benefits of obtaining a green card are that you have the right to both work and live in the U.S. for any employer you choose. You are now considered a full-fledge "immigrant" vs. a "non-immigrant". You are no longer tied to an employer or to a school and can overall come and go as you please although the holder does have to maintain permanent resident status and can be removed if certain conditions of this status are not met.

Also, the Green Card does have an expiration date of 10 years, but it can be extended easily if all general conditions are met. These general conditions are simple and include not committing a crime, not submitting fraudulent application documents, paying your taxes and some other no brainers. Overall if you are a good person you shouldn't have an issue.

While your Green Card application is pending you should obtain two documents that make your life easier while you wait for your official card.

1. Temporary work permit – this is the Employment Authorization Document (EAD) mentioned in earlier chapters and allows you to work legally in the U.S.
2. Temporary Travel Document- this document allows you to re-enter the U.S. while you Green Card application is pending

Now, onto how you can obtain a Green Card. There are 5 ways to obtain a Green Card. Here is the list and then a little further along in this chapter are detailed descriptions of each way to get your Green Card. Please note that for most Green Card applications you cannot initiate the process yourself, it has to be started by your employer or a family member. There are some instances where you can file yourself, but those are not very prevalent.

You may obtain a Green Car:

1. Via a family member
2. Via employment (through company sponsorship)
3. Via your personal investment
4. Via the Diversity or Green Card Lottery
5. Via 'The Registry' provisions of the Immigration and Nationality Act.

Before we get into the details of each path I want to outline the 3 Application Steps.

1. Fill out an immigration petition using Form I-130 and supply all supporting documentation required.
2. Wait for a visa number to be available. There are quotas for each path and country per year so you will have to wait until a visa number is available from the National Visa Center. If your petition though is for an immediate relative there will be no wait time.

3. Wait for your final status adjudication- once your status is finally updated you will receive your Green Card in the mail within a few weeks.

Sponsoring a Family Member

There are a few different ways for a U.S. citizen or, in some cases, Green Card holders to sponsor relatives for Green Cards.

1. Immediate relative petition - An immediate relative petition is for U.S. citizens who are interested in sponsoring one or more immediate relatives to come and live in the U.S. under permanent resident status. Immediate relatives include: spouses, parents and unmarried children under the age of 21. Immediate relatives are granted visa numbers immediately and do not have to wait for one to become available. If he or she is inside the U.S. then he/she should apply to change his status from temporary to permanent as soon as the petition is approved.

2. Preference Petition – This petition is used by relatives to bring over their family members, but can also be used by employers on behalf of employees. (The employer option is discussed in the employment path below.)

   A preference petition can be filed by:
   - A United States citizen on behalf of an unmarried adult child, 21 years of age or older
   - A legal permanent resident for a spouse, unmarried child (under 21 years old) or unmarried adult child.

   Unlike an immediate relative petition, the person petitioned for must wait until a visa number is available. Exact processing times for a preference petition will vary according to the applicant's preference category.

   Preference is given in the following order:

- First Preference: Unmarried, adult (over 21 years old) children of U.S. citizens
- Second Preference: Spouses of lawful permanent residents and unmarried children, regardless of age, of lawful permanent residents and their children
- Third Preference: Married children of U.S. citizens, their spouses and minor children
- Fourth Preference: Brothers and sisters of adult U.S. citizens, their spouses and their minor children.

There are a couple more things to note about sponsoring relatives or being sponsored by relatives.

- Always include documentation with your application clearly showing that you are a U.S. citizen or Green Card holder.
- Always include documentation demonstrating your relationship as family.
- You may file the immigrant visa petition and the application for permanent residency at the same time.
- If sponsoring a family member you will have to prove that you are above the designated income threshold and therefore have the ability to support the relative you are sponsoring at 125% of the mandated poverty line.

Employment Based Sponsorship

If you have an employer that is willing to sponsor you for a Green Card, they will be sponsoring an "employment based" visa, which are classed under the EB visa category. There are currently 5 EB visas, EB-1, EB-2, EB-3, EB-4 and EB-5. There is also a proposed EB-6 for business start ups but that category is still being debated in Congress. Who knows how long that will take.

Here's some more detailed information about what each of these 5 categories is for.

- EB-1 – This visa is for priority workers including foreign nationals with extraordinary abilities, outstanding professors, and certain multinational executives
- EB -2 – This visa is for people holding post graduate degrees like a master's degree, PhD or someone with a bachelor's degree holder and 5+ years of progressive and relevant work experience.
- EB-3 – This visa is for skilled workers, professionals and other qualified workers EB-4 – This visa is certain special immigrants including those in religious vocations
- EB-5 – This visa is for those who wish to invest their own money to start a company in the U.S. and create U.S. based jobs. This visa will be covered in more detail later in this chapter.

EB-2 and EB-3 Visa Process

The EB-2 and EB-3 Immigrant visas are the most common Green Cards for H1B and E3 visa holders to transfer to so let's walk through the process for these in more detail.

Step 1: Labor Certification

During the Labor Certification procedure your employer must prove to the Department of Labor (DOL) that they could not find a suitable person for your specific role within the U.S. Your employer will have to advertise for your position, possibly interview other candidates, and take any other pertinent recruitment steps to prove this under the DOL guidelines.

Your employer will then file Form ETA-750 with the DOL explaining that they were unable to find a suitable candidate and as a result they wish to sponsor you for permanent residency.

Unfortunately this process can take many months or years to complete and does cost the employer money, exactly how much depends on the circumstances, but a conservative estimate is $1000.

Step 2: I-140 to USCIS & Adjustment of Status (I-485)

Once your Labor Certificate is approved your employer will file Form I-140 (known as Petition for Immigrant Worker) on your behalf. The Form I-485 can be filed at the same time, but will not be approved under after your I-140 is accepted. At this point your employer will need to demonstrate that the company is on a solid financial footing and is capable of paying the salary advertised for the job.

The final Adjustment of Status will be approved once a visa number is available. Depending on your country of origin, this could be immediate or take several years. A key restriction at this stage is that the applicant must stay with the company that has applied on his/her behalf. If he leaves the company he will have to start the Green Card process again from the beginning.

One final thing to note about the EB-2/EB-3 process is that spouse and dependent applications can be file once the I-140 is approved for the primary applicant, not before.

So what are the costs associated with an EB-2 or EB-3 visa? The I-140 processing fee currently is $500 for regular and $1000 for premium processing. The I-485 is $93 and there is an additional $120 medical assessment that must be paid to an approved doctor and also an $80 biometric fee. Of course all of these fees are multiplied when dependents and spouses are involved as well. Also, remember that these costs exclude any legal fees you might have. If you decide to enlist the help of an attorney yourself, I can't stress enough that you should find someone that will charge a set fee for the entire Green Card process.

While you are in the application process for an employer based Green Card be aware that if you change companies or even substantially change your role or level within the same company you will have to begin the application process again. This rather unfair rule has lead many people to abandon their Green Card out of frustration with the years of waiting and the fact that many of them have to turn down promotions or great offers elsewhere while they wait for their application to work its way through the process. Streamlining this process would definitely help keep solid immigrant talent in the U.S. and would benefit everyone involved.

EB-5 Visa or Individual Investment

The EB-5 visa is meant for those who wish to invest their own money to start up a company in the U.S. and employ others in the United States as well. There are 10,000 of these visas granted a year and about half of those go to individuals who invest via a designated USCIS Regional Center in a given U.S. state. The Regional Centers advertise heavily encouraging foreigners to create a business in their area and invest their personal funds. They should be assessed with caution as this is the United States and there is no guarantee that any venture will succeed.

Once an investor commits the funds he/she, along with dependents, is granted a 2 year conditional Green Card that can be made permanent following a petition to the USCIS slightly before the 2 year expiration. In this petition, the candidate must prove that both an investment has been made and that at least 10 local jobs have been created as a result of that investment. After 5 more years, assuming the same criteria are still met, the investor and dependents can apply for U.S. citizenship.

For the EB-5 visa there are no education, language or industry requirements, but applicants must pass a mental and physical health check, criminal background check and prove that they acquired the investment funds by legal means. They must also, as always, pay the required fees.

EB-5 Direct Investment vs. Regional Centers/Qualified Investments

The rules for obtaining an EB-5 visa differ depending on if you are directly investing or investing through a Regional Center. The Regional Centers were created to help areas of high unemployment and lesser economic activity by attracting immigrant financed companies to these areas and creating jobs. The regions are rural or have a high unemployment rate that is at least 1.5 times higher than the national average.

If investing through a Regional Center the minimum investment is $500,000 while direct investment has a $1,000,000 minimum. The direct investment path requires a full, and thorough, business plan while the business plan is mostly in place through the Regional Centers. Either way, 10 jobs must still be created for the Green Card to be renewed after 2 years.

Either way you choose to invest there is a risk, but be aware that the USCIS does not have any official statistics on the success rate of the various Regional Centers. It is quite possible for your venture and investment to fail no matter which path you follow.

The Diversity Visa (DV) or Green Card Lottery

The Diversity Visa is a process that randomly grants 55,000 permanent residency visas per year to foreign nationals to come live and work in the U.S. The purpose of the lottery is to ensure a more diverse population base in the U.S. There is NO cost to enter the lottery which is amazing in the U.S. immigration process. Although there is no charge there are plenty of websites that charge you to submit your application for you. THESE SITES ARE SCAMS! You do not need outside help to fill out the application as it is very simple. The only reason help may be required is if your English is not good enough to read the form.

The lottery system works by:
1. Taking applications from early October to early November online ONLY
2. Announcing winners via MAIL only usually from April to July the following year.
3. Applying the visa for the year after winning onward. In other words, if you apply in 2011, you learn of success in 2012 and your visa takes effect in 2013. The DV lottery will be named for the year the visas will take affect, in this example DV-2013.

Now here is the information you will need to provide on our application. As you can see the application is very straightforward and easy to follow.

1. FULL NAME – Last/Family Name, First Name, Middle name
2. DATE OF BIRTH – Day, Month, Year
3. GENDER – Male or Female
4. CITY WHERE YOU WERE BORN
5. COUNTRY WHERE YOU WERE BORN – The name of the country should be that which is currently in Use for the place where you were born.
6. COUNTRY OF ELIGIBILITY OR CHARGEABILITY FOR THE DV PROGRAM – Your country of eligibility will normally be the same as your country of birth. Your country of eligibility is not related to where you live. If you were born in a country that is not eligible for the DV program, please review the instructions to see if there is another option for country chargeability available for you.
7. ENTRY PHOTOGRAPH(S) – See the technical information on photograph specifications. Make sure you include photographs of your spouse and all your children, if applicable.
8. MAILING ADDRESS – In Care Of, Address Line 1, Address Line 2, City/Town, District/Country/Province/State, Postal Code/Zip Code, and Country
9. COUNTRY WHERE YOU LIVE TODAY
10. PHONE NUMBER (optional)
11. E-MAIL ADDRESS (optional)
12. WHAT IS THE HIGHEST LEVEL OF EDUCATION YOU HAVE ACHIEVED, AS OF TODAY? You must indicate which one of the following represents your own highest level of educational achievement: (1) Primary school only, (2) High school, no degree, (3) High school degree, (4) Vocational school, (5) Some university courses, (6) University degree, (7) Some graduate level courses, (8) Master degree, (9) Some doctorate level courses, and (10) Doctorate degree

13. MARITAL STATUS – Unmarried, Married, Divorced, Widowed, or Legally Separated
14. NUMBER OF CHILDREN – Entries MUST include the name, date, and place of birth of your spouse and all natural children, as well as all legally-adopted children and stepchildren who are unmarried and under the age of 21 on the date of your entry (do not include children who are already U.S. citizens or Legal Permanent Residents), even if you are no longer legally married to the child's parent, and even if the spouse or child does not currently reside with you and/or will not immigrate with you. Note that married children and children 21 years or older are not eligible for the diversity visa; however, U.S. law protects children from "aging out" in certain circumstances. If your electronic DV entry is made before your unmarried child turns 21, and the child turns 21 before visa issuance, he/she will be treated as though he/she were under 21 for visa-processing purposes. Failure to list all children who are eligible will result in disqualification of the principal applicant and refusal of all visas in the case at the time of the visa interview.
15. SPOUSE INFORMATION – Name, Date of Birth, Gender, City/Town of Birth, Country of Birth, and Photograph. Failure to list your spouse will result in disqualification of the principal applicant and refusal of all visas in the case at the time of the visa interview.
16. CHILDREN INFORMATION – Name, Date of Birth, Gender, City/Town of Birth, Country of Birth, and Photograph: Include all children declared in #14 above.

Again, it is easy and straightforward. You do not need to use some online service to help you submit your application.

As of 2008 applicants were told that if they kept their confirmation page after submitting the application they could check online sometime after the mid year to see if they won a lottery visa or not. Thus non-winners could for the first time know that they did not receive a visa and apply again for the next year.

One key thing to note before entering the lottery is that you must have either a high school education, its equivalent or 2 years of work experience within the past 5 years in an occupation requiring at least 2 years of training or experience to perform. If you do not meet this requirement then applying for the DV Lottery is futile.

The Registry

The last way to obtain a Green Card is through the Registry, which is a section of immigration law that allows certain people who have resided in the U.S. since January 1, 1972 to apply for a Green Card (permanent residence) even if they are currently in the United States unlawfully.

You may eligible for a Green Card under the registry provision if:

- You entered the United States prior to January 1, 1972
- You have continuously resided in the U.S. since your entry
- You are not ineligible for naturalization (citizenship) or inadmissible due to terrorist activities, criminal actions or security grounds
- You are considered a person of good moral standing
- Never participated in Nazi persecutions or genocide
- Have no other option for becoming a lawful citizen

To apply for a Green Card under the registry provisions you must file Form I-485 and submit the following supporting documentation.

- Two passport style photos
- Form G-325A, Biographic Information
- A copy of government issue identification
- A copy of your birth certificate
- A copy of your passport page with a nonimmigrant visa (if applicable)
- A copy of your passport page with entry stamp(if applicable)
- Form I-94, Arrival/Departure Record (if applicable)
- Evidence that you entered the country prior to January 1, 1972

- Evidence to establish continuous residency in the U.S.

One last thing to note is that you must apply for a registry Green Card at your local USCIS office that has jurisdiction over your current place of residence.

So those are the paths to a Green Card. As you can see there are several ways to obtain your Green Card, but it does take a long time and require a lot of patience. Now let's go on to discuss the Green Card Interview, especially if you are getting a Green Card via marriage.

Green Card Interview- for Spouses

If you are filing for a Green Card solely for yourself you may or may not be called for an interview, but if you and your spouse are applying you will undoubtedly be called for an interview. The point of this interview is to establish that your relationship is genuine and that you did not get married solely for the sake of getting a Green Card. If your marriage is genuine, you truly should have no problems, but it is still best to be prepared.

Be prepared for your interview by providing all the requested documents and by learning about the process. The USCIS is going to dig deep into your relationship with their questions. Although no one can predict what you will be asked here are some questions you should be prepared to answer.

1. What are your plans for the future for both of you
2. Detailed questions regarding the veracity of your Green Card application
3. Your individual interests, hobbies or pastimes and the same for your spouse or fiancé
4. How you met your spouse or fiancé
5. Your work history and current work situation
6. Just about any question pertaining to your life and relationship

The USCIS consular officer's main goal is understanding your relationship and ensuring that the marriage is valid. The questions may seem arbitrary at times, but the point is to get consistent answers from both parties. If you answer questions in truly contradictory ways the officer may become concerned and ask even more pointed questions. Make sure to answer every question as honestly and openly as possible. Do not lie!

Part of the interview will focus on specific documents. You should have received a list of requested documentation when your interview was arranged. Make sure you bring them all with you. Some of the common items requested during this interview are:

1. Your green card appointment letter
2. Your passport that will be valid for at least the next six months
3. Alien registration form DS-230 and your application for green card
4. Birth certificates
5. A marriage certificate, if applicable
6. Divorce certificates
7. Two front view – and recent – photographs
8. Any relevant USCIS documentation
9. Death certificates

Truly, if your marriage is valid and not solely for the purpose of obtaining a Green Card your interview should go very smoothly and your Green Card should be approved.

Renewal Process

A permanent resident card is normally valid for ten years. As you near its expiration date you will need to go through the Green Card renewal process by filing Form I-90, Application to Replace Permanent Resident Card with the USCIS.

As you come up for renewal you should apply at least 6 months before the expiry date. While your card is being renewed you will receive a temporary proof of status, which provides evidence of your residence in the U.S. while your card is being processed. It is good for a year and you should receive your renewed Green Card in 10 to 12 months after your initial application.

When applying, make sure to research the different renewal forms and select the proper one for your renewal reason. There are different forms based on circumstances such as lost or mutilated card, card expiring, an address change, etc. All of these reasons may have a different form to file so check out the forms online and select the proper one for your situation. Also make sure to check out your version of Green Card as some actually have no expiration date, although most will be 10 years.

So how much does all this cost you ask. The basic renewal fee is $110. If you have other additional special needs for your card additional fees may be required, but that is not generally the case. If you file for renewal after your card is past due there will be additional fees as well. If you do not have the money for the fees you can apply for a waiver, but you will need to go to your local USCIS office in person to do it.

Conditional Green Card

A conditional Green Card is one that is valid for only two years. A conditional Green Card cannot be renewed. Conditional Green Card holders must have the conditions removed during the 90 day period before the card expires since if the conditions are not removed they will lose their status when the card expires. Assuming your application is approved the conditions will be removed and you will receive a permanent resident card that will be valid for the next ten years.

There are many reasons why a conditional Green Card might be issued, but the two main ones are: you obtained your Green Card via marriage or you invested significant money into a U.S. based business as your means to obtain a Green Card. As discussed earlier under the EB-5 visa section you can have your conditions removed if you are an investor by demonstrating that your company is financially solid and that you have created at least 10 jobs within the

U.S. You will have to file Form I-751 for removal of conditions and will need to provide the following supporting documents.

- Copy of the front and back of your Permanent Resident Card.
- Evidences to prove that your marriage is legitimate.
- Evidences for seeking a waiver (If filing to waive the joint filing requirement)
- Court order if you have changed your name legally.
- English translation of all foreign language documents from an authorized translator.

If your conditional Green Card was issued due to your marriage to a U.S. Citizen you will need to prove your marriage is legitimate before the two years expire. To prove your marriage is legitimate submit some or all of the following documents.

- Copy of your marriage certificate.
- Copy of birth certificates of the children you have had together.
- Documents of Joint ownership or property such as financial records of assets, federal tax return, insurance policies.
- Rental receipts of all the apartments that you have occupied together.
- Affidavits from at-least two people, who have personally known you and your spouse from the time the conditional residence was granted. The person who signs the Affidavit should witness before the immigration officer that whatever is written in the Affidavit is true.

Visa Retrogression

Visa retrogression is one of the more difficult topics for most people to understand. The main point of retrogression is that the U.S. government makes only a set amount of immigrant visas (green cards) available per year. These visas are then allocated among various immigrant visa categories and countries. If the number of immigrants approved for a specific immigrant visa category is greater than the number of visa numbers being issued that year, a backlog is created. This backlog is called a retrogression of visa numbers. What this means for the applicant is that they have to "wait in line" until a visa number becomes available. The visa numbers are given out on a first come, first served policy.

The date the applicant begins the Green Card process is the date that becomes their "priority date". This date is important because it determines the order in which that person receives a visa number. If visa numbers retrogress there will not be one available for the applicant until their priority date is reached in the overall process. If your visa category does retrogress it can be very frustrating as you won't know for sure when yours will be approved. The best piece of advice I can give is to sit tight and wait. Your Green Card will come through with time.

My Green Card is Pending- How Can I Work?

Now that we've discussed visa retrogression one of the next questions will of course be, "Wait a minute, if I have to wait for a free visa number how do I keep working?" Well, you can file Form I-765, application for employment authorization, along with your status application. Along with the I-765 you will also have to submit a copy of your I-94, Arrival Departure Card. Once your application is approved by the USCIS you should receive an EAD card within 90 days which will allow you to keep working in the U.S. while your Green Card is pending.

If you file form I-765 at the same time as your application for a Green Card there is no additional cost. Yes, that's right one more thing that you don't have to pay for. There aren't many of those so be grateful. It is highly recommended to file the I-765 with the I-485 (Green Card application) at the same time to save money, allow you to work while your application is pending and also because it facilitates easier processing of the application.

You can check the status of your I-765 Form online and if for any reason your request is denied you will receive a letter from the USCIS outlining exactly why your application was rejected. You are then allowed to request that the USCIS officers reconsider your case.

There is a ton of paperwork to this whole process, but if you stay on top of it you will be able to work in the U.S. even while your Green Card status is pending. Make sure you keep records and follow up on the process if you are not notified in a timely manner of where your applications and petitions stand.

Traveling Outside the U.S.

Once you have your Green card you are overall expected to reside in the U.S. If you plan to be outside the U.S. for more than a year, you might raise a few eyebrows at the border when you attempt to re-enter. To avoid this issue you simply need to apply for a re-entry permit if you will be traveling outside the U.S. for over 6 months. If you do not apply for this re-entry permit immigration officials may think that you intended to abandon your permanent residency status and place you in removal proceedings.

A re-entry permit demonstrates that you did not intend to abandon your status while being abroad and it allows you to re-enter the U.S. easily after a long time abroad without having to obtain a returning resident visa. The USCIS defines a long time abroad as 2 years, but it is always good to be on the safe side and apply for one if you are gone for 6 months or more. The re-entry permit is valid for 2 years from date of issuance.

Although two years is technically the limit, if you are out of the country for over 6 months you should be prepared to answer questions as to why. There are exceptions for extenuating circumstances such as a serious illness or issues with children, but exceptions are fairly rare.

To apply for a re-entry permit file Form I-131 and don't forget the fees ($385) associated with it to the USCIS. Ensure that you file it at least 60 days before you intend to travel. Also note that you need to be physically present in the U.S. to file this form and cannot file it from overseas. The USCIS technically states that you do not need to file this form if you will be away from the U.S. for less than a year.

There are generally only 2 reasons why the I-131 Form is not approved:

1. You already have a valid, approved re-entry permit,
2. The federal register contains a notice that prohibits the issuance of a re-entry permit for travel to the area where you intend to visit.

Besides those reasons, re-entry permits are easily granted as long as there is no issue with your status.

How to Lose Your Permanent Resident Status

After receiving permanent resident status it is fairly tough to lose this status as long as you are a decent person. Since it is a difficult, drawn out process to become a permanent resident of the United States you should take care not to do anything that would jeopardize your status. It truly can take only moments to undo all that you have worked so hard for.

The easiest way to lose your status is to engage in any form of criminal activity. If you are convicted of a crime or practice activities that are considered a crime in the U.S., or any other country, your status will probably be revoked on the spot. You would be instantly deported and will not be permitted to enter the U.S. ever again.

Here is a list of some rather obvious crimes that will get you deported.

- Committing murder.
- Activities involving terror which would may pose a threat to the local population.
- Rape, molestation and sexually assaulting women and children.
- Illegal dealings in arms, drugs and human trafficking.
- Sexual misconduct, causing physical harm
- Any fraudulent practices which have led to loss or damage to people and property.

- Threatening someone for one's own means as well as reckless behavior.
- Any form of violent activities and the punishment of such crimes include a minimum of a year of service in the prison.

Additionally the following actions will also have serious ramifications and will probably result in loss of status and deportation.

- Providing false information and/or lying to get immigration benefits.
- Claiming to be a citizen of the United States when not.
- Participating in elections – federal or local, that is only permitted for citizens of the United States.
- Indulging in drinking or being a habitual drunk as defined by the U.S. immigrant department as well as using drugs illegally.
- Being married to two people at the same time.
- Neglecting the responsibilities of supporting the family.
- Found to be practicing domestic violence.
- Not filing tax returns on time.

If you commit any of the above mentioned actions or crimes you should contact an immigration attorney or community based organization as they may be able to help you. That being said, the U.S. is quite strict on crimes committed by immigrants so do not expect any leniency. The best thing to do is to lead a good and crime free life.

Chapter 8: U.S. Citizenship

Thanks to the United States Constitution there are 3 ways to become a United States Citizen.

1. JU.S. soli, or right of birthplace: meaning that any child born in the U.S. is automatically a U.S. Citizen, even if the child's mother was in the U.S. illegally. This provision does not apply to a child of a foreign diplomat at time of birth.
2. JU.S. sanguinis, or right of blood: meaning that if a child is born outside the U.S. to parents who are United States citizens that child is a U.S. citizen.
3. Naturalization: meaning that anyone not granted citizenship at birth can follow this process to obtain U.S. citizenship later in life.

Although all three of these paths can make someone a citizen of the United States this chapter is going to focus on Naturalization as that is the process for someone to immigrate to the U.S. and eventually become a full-fledged citizen.

Naturalization Eligibility

So now that you've been a permanent U.S. resident for a number of years you may be considering becoming a full-fledged U.S. citizen. For many immigrants becoming a citizen of the United States is a dream come true. To become a citizen you first have to make sure you are eligible. You may be eligible to obtain U.S. Citizenship if:

- You are an immigrant with five years permanent residence in the U.S. and at least half that time you were physically present in the U.S. with no periods outside the country for over six months
- You are currently married to a U.S. citizen, have been married to that citizen for the past three years and have been a permanent resident for at least three years
- You served in the U.S. Armed Forces for at least three years

- You honorably completed active duty military service in the U.S. Armed Forces during:
    - World War I (November 11, 1916 - April 6, 1917)**
    - World War II (September 1, 1939 - December 31, 1946)**
    - Korea (June 25, 1950 - July 1, 1955)**
    - Vietnam (February 28, 1961 - October 15, 1978) or
    - Persian Gulf (August 2, 1990 - April 11, 1991)
    - Persian Gulf (September 11, 2001 - Present)

    **Note: I realize that some of these dates (and wars) were so long ago at this point that the chances of someone who served during those times applying for citizenship now are remote. It's included for those who are interested.

- You were married to a U.S. citizen who died during honorable active duty service in the U.S. Armed Forces
- You have been a permanent resident for the past five years and meet one of the following requirements:
    - You are an employee or a contractor to the U.S. Government
    - You perform ministerial or priestly functions for a religious denomination or an interdenominational organization with a valid presence in the U.S.
    *Note: Spouses of these individuals are also eligible.

- You are the spouse of a U.S. citizen who meets one of the following criteria:
    - A member of the U.S. Armed Forces
    - An employee of an American research institution recognized by the Attorney General
    - A public international organization employee which the United States is a member of via law or treaty
    - An employee of an American-owned firm that seeks the development of United States' foreign trade and commerce interests

USCIS General Requirements

Above are very specific reasons why you may be eligible to become a naturalized U.S. Citizen. Hopefully you fall under one of these categories and are able to continue the naturalization process. Assuming you are eligible under one of these categories there are still some basic requirements that you must meet in order to become a citizen. None of these requirements is difficult to understand or meet, but they are important. If you do not meet these requirements your application will almost certainly be rejected. Let's walk through these requirements now.

- You must be at least 18 years old.
- You must be a lawful, permanent resident of the United States.
- If you are married to a U.S. citizen, you can apply for U.S. citizenship after three years of residence in the United States. All others can apply for citizenship only after five years. At least half of this time (3 or 5 years) must have been spent physically in the U.S.
- You have resided in the U.S. from the time you filed your application for U.S. citizenship.
- You must take an oath of allegiance to the U.S. constitution.
- You must have proficient fluency in English. (This requirement may be waived under some circumstances.)
- You must have sufficient knowledge of the history, role and functioning of the U.S. government.
- You must not have a criminal history
- You must meet the continuous physical presence requirements as outlined below

As with everything in the U.S. immigration process there are rules and even more rules for becoming a U.S. citizen. Besides the basic requirements outlined above there are more rigorous and detailed physical presence requirements that vary based on whether or not you are married to a U.S. citizen or not. These additional physical presence requirements must be met in order for you to continue your path to citizenship.

First, here are the requirements if you are married to a U.S. citizen and applying for U.S. citizenship based on that marriage.

- You must physically live with your spouse.
- You must have lived with your spouse for at least three years before you apply for U.S. citizenship.
- You must have physically resided in the U.S. for at least 18 months.
- You must have resided continuously in the state you are applying from for at least the past three months.
- Your spouse must remain a U.S. citizen from the time you applied for citizenship until the date of your naturalization examination.

Now, if you are not married to a U.S. citizen there are two physical presence requirements you must meet besides the requirement that you must be a permanent resident for at least five years.

- You must have been physically present in the U.S. for at least 30 months.
- You must have resided in the state you are applying from continuously for at least the past three months.

You should take note that physical presence is different from continuous residence. Physical presence means that you were literally in the country while continuous residence means that you lawfully resided in the U.S. without any long absences. If you are physically outside the U.S. for more than one year you will lose your continuous residence requirements of three or five years, depending on marriage, unless the absence is excused by the U.S. government. Exceptions are sometimes made for circumstances such as illness or tending to a minor child.

Naturalization Process

The path to citizenship differs based on whether or not you are an adult (over 18) or a child (under 18). First, I want to walk you through the naturalization process for an adult then we will focus on how a child may become a U.S. citizen.

If you are an adult then you need to file Form N-600 with the USCIS. The fee for filing this form is a steep $600 so make sure you check and double check that you filled it out accurately and completely. You will need to submit the following supporting documents with the completed N-600:

- Your birth certificate
- Marriage certificate(s), if applicable
- Marriage termination document(s), if applicable
- Copy of Permanent Resident Card (Green Card)
- Proof or required residence and physical residence within the United States
- Evidence of any legal name changes, if applicable
- 2 passport style photographs.

Once the USCIS has received your application they will contact you to let you know where you can get fingerprinted. Being fingerprinted is a requirement for the naturalization process.

Processing time for your naturalization application will vary depending on the area in which you live. An exact timeframe is not given. As your application begins to move through the process you will be contacted for a Naturalization Interview. For your interview go to your local USCIS at the specified time and bring state-issued identification, such as a driver's license, your EAD Card and any other documents requested. During the interview you will be asked questions about your application and your background. Answer honestly. You will then be asked to take an English test and a U.S. government civics test.

After completing your interview and your tests you will be given the results and told if you will receive U.S. citizenship or not. Hopefully it is good news!

Assuming you have passed your interview and the tests you will be given a date to attend your Naturalization Ceremony where you will officially become an American citizen. Congratulations! At the ceremony you will be asked to return your Permanent Residency Card, answer some questions about what you have done since your interview (they are most interested in ascertaining if you have left the country or not) and you will take the Oath of Allegiance. You are then an official citizen of the United States and will be given your Certificate of Naturalization. It's definitely time for a celebration so go have some fun.

U.S. Citizenship for Children

Children, under the age of 18, may not become U.S. citizens through the naturalization process. If they need to follow the naturalization process they must wait until they are 18 years of age. They may then file for citizenship and follow the process outlined above.

If the child was born in the U.S.; however, the process is very simple. They merely have to produce their birth certificate and they will then be able to obtain other governmental documents such as a passport.

If the child was born outside the U.S. and at least one parent was a U.S. citizen at the time of birth, whether by birth or naturalization, the child may file for citizenship by using the N-600 form. There are a few more requirements you must meet to be eligible for citizenship so let's list those here.

- You must reside in the U.S. in the legal and physical custody of your U.S. citizen parent and must be eligible for lawful admission for permanent residence.
- To qualify as a "child" you must be unmarried. If you were born out of wedlock you must have be "legitimized" when you were under 16 and in the legal custody of the legitimizing parent. Note, that if you are a stepchild who was not adopted, you will not qualify for citizenship purposes.

If you meet the above requirements you qualify for U.S. citizenship without having to file an application; however, if you want to document your citizenship status you have to file Form N-600.

If you are a biological or adopted child of a U.S. citizen, but you regularly reside abroad you can still qualify for citizenship, but there are additional requirements. The best thing to do in this situation is to do research on the USCIS website or speak to a USCIS official directly.

The MAVNI Program

I'm willing to bet that you've never heard of MAVNI before basically because neither had I until fairly recently. MAVNI stands for Military Accessions Vital to the National Interest and was started in November 2008 when the then U.S. Secretary of Defense, Robert Gates, signed a memorandum authorizing a new program to allow non citizens of the United States already in the country legally to join the military and apply immediately for, and get U.S. citizenship within six months.

The idea was initiated in 2002 after the U.S. military war in Iraq in order to increase recruiting efforts and to encourage people who spoke 35 specific languages to enlist in the military in exchange for a fast route to citizenship. As of right now the program is currently on hold, but it is expected to be started up again, but no one knows exactly when.

The basic requirements for the MAVNI Program are:

- The applicant must be in the U.S. legally.
- The applicant must be able to provide legal documents demonstrating he or she is in the U.S. legally.
- The applicant must be able to speak one of the 35 specific languages fluently. Most of the languages are Asian or Middle Eastern with a few additional Eastern European languages.
- Students on visas that meet the other requirements are also eligible.

The army will help any new recruits with their application and also assist any family members with their applications as well. The military will provide the needed guidance and will also waive the application fee of $625. Not bad, if you are willing to serve in the U.S. armed forces.

Common Myths

Before I wrap up this book there are 5 common myths surrounding U.S. Citizenship that I wish to dispel. It is true that the U.S. immigration process is a long, maze-like mess that can take way too may years and way too much money to navigate. That being said the naturalization process is actually fairly straightforward. That being said, the following incorrect myths definitely do not help the immigrant to find his/her way through the naturalization process.

Here are the 5 most common myths:

- If an immigrant marries a U.S. citizen he/she is automatically granted citizenship. In truth, if you marry a U.S. citizen you still need to follow the USCIS procedures by applying for a marriage based visa and proving the validity of your marriage.
- An immigrant is able to bring a child into the U.S. only if he/she is married. That is not true. Children are able to relocate to the U.S. under a family sponsored visa regardless of your marital status.
- The Naturalization Process is easy. Now, this one is especially funny as the truth is that the naturalization process, although straightforward, is complex and has numerous steps that must be followed.
- The naturalization test is really simple. In truth the naturalization test is a civics test covering U.S. history and the U.S. government. It requires a significant amount of knowledge and you should study.
- You must be able to speak and write English to become a U.S. citizen. Although, in most situations this is true, there are cases where you will be able to become a naturalized

citizen even if you are unable to read or write English fluently.

Overall the U.S. naturalization process is straightforward and fairly easy to understand. That being said it does have many steps and procedures that you need to follow. If you are unsure about how to follow the process then you may wish to retain the services of a lawyer. Of course, make sure the lawyer is competent and it is recommended that you find one who will work on a fixed retainer rather than on an hourly basis.

I hope this book has helped you to understand some of the U.S. immigration process and procedures. It obviously does not cover all the visa types in detail and cannot list every single rule and regulation for U.S. immigration. To obtain even more detailed information visit the USCIS website at http://www.uscis.gov.

Best of luck in your journey to your dreams!

Made in the USA
Lexington, KY
18 August 2012